678910111213141516171819202122232425262728293031323334353637383940414243444546474849505152535455565758596061626364656667686970717273747576777879808

The Harper's Index Book

891011121314151617181920212223242526272829303132333435363738394041424344454647484950515253545556575859606162636465666768697071727374757677787980818 2

THE
HARPER'S
INDEX BOOK

789101112131415161718192021222324252627282930313233343536373839404142434445464748495051525354555657585960616263646566676869707172737475767778798081

VOLUME 3

Edited by Charis Conn & Lewis H. Lapham

Introduction by George Plimpton

FRANKLIN
SQUARE
PRESS

PREVIOUS HARPER'S INDEX COLLECTIONS:
The Harper's Index Book (Henry Holt, 1986)
What Counts (Henry Holt, 1991)

Published by Franklin Square Press, a division of
Harper's Magazine, 666 Broadway, New York, NY 10012

First edition
First printing 2000

LIBRARY OF CONGRESS CATALOGING-IN-PUBLICATION DATA

The Harper's index book / edited by Charis Conn & Lewis H. Lapham ;
introduction by George Plimpton. — 1st ed.
    p. cm.
    "Volume three."
    Includes index.
    ISBN 1-879957-54-X (pbk.: alk. paper)
    1. Handbooks, vade-mecums, etc. 2. Statistics. I. Conn, Charis.
II. Lapham, Lewis H. III. Harper's magazine.
AG105.H355 2000
031.02 — dc21   00-056150

Manufactured in the United States of America.

This book has been produced on acid-free paper.

Designed by Lindgren/Fuller Design

10 9 8 7 6 5 4 3 2 1

Contents

Contents

Acknowledgments

The compilation of this book, like that of the monthly *Harper's* Index, required the collective skills and diligence of many people, including the magazine's entire staff. For his help in the monumental task of reviewing and refining several thousand statistics, the editors would like to thank John Cook. We also wish to thank our colleagues Margaret Cordi, Rachel A. Monahan, and Mary J. LaMotte for their invaluable patience, attention to detail, and intelligence in organizing and revising the manuscript. For intrepidly rechecking several years' worth of *Harper's* Indexes, as well as unearthing new and worthy materials, we are grateful to our fine research team: Carin Besser, Keith Donoghue, Will Vladeck Heinrich, Sarah Moffat Lorimer, David Miller, Jebediah Reed, Lewis G. Robinson, J. R. Romanko, Sarah Smith, and Sarah C. Vos. Special thanks to *Harper's Magazine* publisher Rick MacArthur for making it all possible; to Laura Lindgren and Celia Fuller for their thoughtful design and scheduling solutions; to Roger Hodge for creating the Index database and shepherding it through its first years; to Donovan Hohn and Clara Jeffery for their tireless aid and wisdom in compiling each month's Index; to Lynn Carlson, Ellen Ryder, Ellen Rosenbush, and Angela Riechers for their steadfast support; and to the hundreds of unpaid interns without whose energies the *Harper's* Index would not exist—this book is for them.

Introduction

I note with great pleasure that this Index has an index—an inspired editorial decision. Not enough has been said in praise of indexes (much less an index to an index) and yet who has not given a sigh of relief upon receiving a weighty tome to find that it includes an index and who has not emitted a groan of despair when it doesn't. The index is, of course, of particular use to critics and reviewers who need only to browse about in it until they find enough references to write what appears on the surface to be a "thorough and authoritative" book review. It is to the point that one of the statistics in the previous edition of the Index book bears this out: it states that 36 percent of reviewers say it is ethical to review a book that they have not finished. The chances are surely that those 36 percent are index browsers.

The index is, of course, essential for historians, politicians, the celebrated, who peek quickly (often in the bookstore itself) to see if they are listed. In literary circles, one remembers the oft told story that Norman Podhoretz saw to this addiction: before presenting a copy of his memoir *Making It* to Norman Mailer, he penciled in beside his friend's name in the index: "Hi Norman!"

Nonfiction writers crave an index to their work—it offers substance. In my own case, a book I wrote about boxing (*Shadowbox*) includes an index whose first five references include Aadland, Beverly; Aaron, Henry; Abernathy, Ralph; Addams, Charles; and Aeschylus. I like to think that this arc of names—a sixteen-year-old girl who danced naked in front of Errol Flynn, a home-run hitter, a civil rights leader, a *New Yorker* cartoonist, a Greek tragedian—suggests a great breadth of knowledge, which, of course, I don't have at all. Nonetheless, on the rare occasions I pick up the book, I always check the index. It makes me feel better.

An Index's index is invariably good browsing, if often startling. The word "motherfucker" pops up in the index of the second edition of the Index book. It turns out that Miles Davis, the jazz trumpeter, uses the word 333 times in his autobiography, which tells us as much about his state of mind as one would want to know.

A word about the Index's history. Lewis Lapham, the present editor of *Harper's*, hit upon the idea of the Index (and its index) while revising the magazine's format in 1983. Toward the end of his career as a columnist for the *Washington Post* he had written what the French call an *amuse*—an imaginary index, composed of categories balanced in comic juxtaposition:

barrels of oil spilled on the beach in Santa Monica
barrels of perfume imported into Atlantic City
mice cloned
currencies devalued by more than 30 percent
politicians (male) currently under criminal indictment
characters (female) killed on prime-time television
missile systems sold to Spanish-speaking dictators
public executions in Tehran
books proscribed in central Ohio
actors drowned at sea

The thought crossed his mind when he took over *Harper's* editorship that perhaps truth was indeed stranger than fiction. His staff went to work. The magazine's first Index appeared in March 1984—the leading entry on the list: Total hours of television watched in American households in 1983: 213,000,000,000.

The Index was an immediate success. It appeared in whole or in part in a large number of magazines and newspapers around the world. Many magazines, *Time*, *Newsweek*, and *Sports Illustrated* among them, have copied the form. They have their own statisticians and researchers casting lines into what Lapham refers to as an "infinite sea of numbers and events."

And what a sea it is. And how little has not been plumbed. In his foreword to the second Index book, Mr. Lapham states: "The age of faith counted the number of angels who danced on the head of a pin." Sure enough! The exact number (according to the American Institute of Physics) turns up in the present volume: 10^{64}, along with the additional information that dancing Rockettes-style, the row across the diameter would total 10^{32} angels.

Out of curiosity I looked up "angel" in the index of the previous Index book to find that the single entry informs us that 74 percent of American teenagers believe in their existence, presumably in a form somewhat more substantial than those enumerated cavorting on the heads of pins!

As Mr. Lapham puts it succinctly, "Numbers can be made to tell as many stories as a crooked lawyer or an old comedian." The entries in the Index, a single line followed by a number, suggest an espousal of the Ernest Hemingway "iceberg" principle of writing, which is that there is seven eighths underwater for every part that shows. Take an example from the first edition of the Index book: "Bottles of Scotch imported by the Ethiopian government to celebrate its tenth anniversary: 480,000." The mind reels! A volume could be written about this. Who ordered the Scotch? Who persuaded the government officials to do such a thing? What sort of parties took place? What policy decisions were made during the binges? How many tons of bicarbonate of soda were consumed to handle the hangovers?

Another example from the present volume: "The largest soap bubble ever recorded: 105 feet." That's a third the length of a football field! Who blew the thing? A large-lunged man? A machine? Did the bubble meander off? What finally popped it? A church steeple? An inquisitive dog's nose?

Another: 2,400 qualifiers refused to join the Phi Beta Kappa Society in 1991. What on earth persuaded these scholars that they shouldn't join? Did they somehow think they were being pledged to a beer-swilling frat house, or even worse, that they were being coerced into an offshoot of the Kappa Kappa Kappa (KKK) and required to wear white shrouds with conical hoods?

Oddly, for all their intrinsic value, I suspect almost all the entries in the Index are in fact "conversation stoppers." The editors urge them on readers for use in starting a discussion at, say, a cocktail party, but it is hard to imagine that if an Index devotee broke into a lull in the cocktail conversation by announcing, "Hey, thirteen minor planets have been named after rock musicians" that the response, accompanied by a puzzled look, wouldn't be, "Well, isn't that interesting," followed by another foot-shuffling lull. If the devotee then tried again ("Hey, 362,000 tons of U.S. chicken feet are exported annually to China"), I suspect the guests would begin to sidle away. Best, I think, to consider these things in Wordsworthian tranquility.

And how absorbing that is! I didn't know that Don King, the boxing promoter, two months after he was acquitted of fraud, took his jurors on vacation to the Bahamas. Nor did I know that the number of objects made with human dung in the permanent collection of the Brooklyn Museum is four. I didn't know that Chicago is by no means the windiest city: it ranks fifty-third. I didn't know that in twenty-six hours you can lose a "Long Island" accent.

There are statistics that dismay: the percentage by which the cost of producing *Titanic* exceeds the 1997 budget of the National Endowment of the Arts: 100. There are those that confound: 2,652 Russian soldiers die every year from suicide or hazing (there's a Gogolian saga!). There are those that delight: New York ranks number one among the urban habitats with the largest peregrine falcon populations. Some of the entries are hard to believe: one out of every three Americans, say, can't name a country against which the USA fought in World War II.

The compilers of the Index go to great lengths to verify their statistics, though quick to mention (in the introduction to the previous edition) Disraeli's familiar dictum: "There are three kinds of lies—lies, damn lies, and statistics."

Some of the more astounding claims (what Mark Twain might refer to as "stretchers") are qualified by such phrases as "said to be..." or "Chances that...."

No matter. As has been suggested, the charm of the Index is that its items so often beg for answers. Often the issues are important and of public concern, worthy of pursuit. Editorial writers, scriptwriters, cartoonists, barroom prophets, nay sayers, fortune-tellers, global strategists, apologists, city planners, mugwumps, soothsayers would be wise to rush posthaste to browse in the Index and its index. Food for thought? A veritable groaning board!

At some point perusing the Index (or its index) I wondered if there was anything numerically of interest in my own life that might be included in future editions. Two possibilities came to mind—1) that I have never knowingly eaten an olive or 2) never had a stick of chewing gum. Nothing under olive. Two references under gum—1) that 39 gallons of the stuff is annually scraped off the grounds of the Statue of Liberty by its maintenance crew, and 2) that the maximum fine for selling chewing gum in Singapore is $1,176. This latter, somewhat odd entry suggests that I am in good company in the non–gum-chewing department. So that leaves olive as a possibility. I shall eagerly seek for it in the next edition.

CIVICS

School Days

Higher Education

Voters and Voting

The Campaign Trail

The White House

The Congress

The Courts

Crime

Punishment

School Days

Number of Los Angeles high school students who earned a varsity letter in comedy in 1998 : 362

Percentage of Americans who believe that career preparation should begin in elementary school : 18

Chance that a U.S. high school student owns a promotional item from a cigarette company : 1 in 3

Percentage of public-high-school teachers who favor banning students from kissing and hugging on school grounds : 69

Percentage of Americans who believe that sex education should be a required school subject : 60

Percentage who believe that the teaching of evolution should be required : 28

Ratio of federal spending each day on a U.S. public-school student to the amount spent on a federal prisoner : 1:4

Minimum amount of salsa that USDA regulations allow a public school to offer as a serving of vegetables, in tablespoons : 2

Number of U.S. public schools that own their own Taco Bell : 220

Days a Denver school principal was put on leave in 1998 for allowing junior-high-school students a sip of wine on a trip to Paris : 13

Days an Ohio public school suspended a fourteen-year-old girl in 1996 for giving a Midol tablet to her classmate : 80

Average number of public-school students expelled for firearm possession each day of the 1997–98 school year : 22

Chance that the murder of a student at a U.S. school between August 1997 and August 1999 was caused by beating, strangling, or knife wounds : 1 in 4

Chance that a U.S. public high school has at least one police officer stationed there full-time : 1 in 5

Percentage change since 1990 in the number of U.S. high school students enrolled in Junior ROTC : +95

Chance that a Chicago high school student is : 1 in 11

Percentage of the murders of U.S. children in 1996 that took place at school : 0.4

Chance that a U.S. student death at school in the 1998 school year was a suicide : 1 in 5

Ratio of U.S. students killed in or near schools in the 1998 school year to those killed in the 1992 school year : 1:2

Chance that an American murdered at school between 1996 and 1998 was a girl : 1 in 4

Chance of this between 1992 and 1994 : 1 in 20

Number of times in 1998 that one New Jersey high school was evacuated due to bomb threats : 30

Chance that a U.S. public school building is in need of "extensive repairs or replacement" : 1 in 3

Chance that a New York City public school was heated with coal in 1995 : 1 in 4

Chance in 1999 : 1 in 4

Chance that a gay Massachusetts teenager reported being threatened or injured at school in 1997 : 1 in 4

Number of U.S. high schools that have hired a Massachusetts firm to test students' hair for evidence of drug use : 80

Chance that a public-high-school student is taught physical sciences by a teacher without a science background : 1 in 2

Percentage of professors of college freshmen and sophomores who believe a diploma from the local public high school guarantees basic skills : 33

Percentage of parents and high school students, respectively, who believe a diploma from the local public high school guarantees basic math and reading skills : 32, 22

Percentage change since 1960 in the number of Americans who belong to a Parent-Teacher Association : −46

Margin by which the ten-member Kansas Board of Education voted to drop human evolution from the curriculum in 1999 : 2

Higher Education

Number of U.S. colleges offering an academic course in "leadership" in 1998 : 237

Percentage of full-time U.S. undergraduates who are over the age of twenty-two : 34

Percentage of U.S. universities that used student evaluations as a factor in granting tenure in 1973 : 23

Percentage that do so today : 88

Minimum number of students invited to join Phi Beta Kappa in 1998 who did not accept : 2,400

Distance, in feet, between the Stanford dorm rooms of Chelsea Clinton and Carolyn Starr, daughter of Kenneth, during the 1998–99 school year : 3,696

Rank of Hillary Clinton and their mothers among the most popular role models for first-year female college students : 2,1

Rank of Bill Gates and Adam Sandler among the most popular role models for first-year male college students : 2,1

Percentage change between 1986 and 1996 in the number of computer-science degrees conferred in the U.S. : –42

Number of the 664 computer-science faculty members at the nation's 28 highest-ranked universities who are black : 8

Number in 1996 : 0

Percentage of grades given at Princeton University between 1992 and 1998 that were As or Bs : 85

Percentage between 1973 and 1977 : 69

Size of a federal grant awarded to Cornell University in 1995 to create an "O. J. Simpson Trial Archive" : $17,000

Number of Harvard law students required to read *Juice: The O. J. Simpson Tragedy* in 1994 : 550

Percentage of Harvard and Michigan law students who said in 1999 that racial diversity in the classroom changed their views on civil rights : 87

Percentage of Americans of English ancestry who are college graduates : 28

Percentage of Americans of Russian ancestry who are : 49

Factor by which Harvard's admission rate for the children of alumni exceeds that for other qualified applicants : 3.63

Percentage change during the 1990s, in real dollars, in the average tuition at a U.S. private college : +24

Percentage change in the average tuition at a public college : +36

Number of Harvard fellowships endowed since 1992 by relatives of suspected terrorist Osama Bin Laden : 2

Number of Ho Chi Minh scholarships awarded to students by a New York City community college during the 1994 school year : 25

Estimated rounds of ammunition bought by the City University of New York since 1995 to train its security force : 110,000

Percentage change since 1966 in the number of U.S. college freshmen who say it is important to follow politics : −50

Percentage change since 1997 in U.S. corporate investment in university-based science and engineering research : +490

Chance that a president of one of the nation's fifty top-ranked universities serves on at least one corporate board : 1 in 2

Number of classes in popular culture taught at the Smithsonian during the summer of 1995 by the PR director of *People* magazine : 6

Voters and Voting

Ratio of Californians who voted to legalize medical marijuana in 1996 to those who voted for Bill Clinton that year : 21:20

Percentage change since 1992 in the number of Latinos registered to vote in California : +52

Chance that a Texan who registered to vote during the first six months of the state's Motor-Voter law did so in a welfare office : 1 in 5

Chances that a Texan who registered to vote during the first six months of welfare reform did : 3 in 50

Percentage change between 1994 and 1998 in the number of votes cast by members of union households : +66

Percentage change during that period in the number of Republican candidates endorsed by a union : +125

Points by which the percentage of Americans with a household income below $10,000 who voted in 1992's presidential election exceeded the percentage who voted in 1996 : 7

Chance that an African-American man was ineligible to vote in 1998 due to former or current imprisonment : 1 in 8

Chance that a southern Republican primary voter who said in 1996 that Pat Buchanan was "too extreme" also voted for him that year : 1 in 25

Ratio of the number of Republicans who said in 1995 that Bob Dole was too conservative to those who said he was not conservative enough : 1:1

Percentage of U.S. voters who said in the spring of 1996 that there was "no chance whatsoever" that they would vote for Bob Dole : 49

Chances that an American is willing to vote for a Mormon for president : 4 in 5

Chance that an American is willing to vote for an atheist : 1 in 2

Percentage points by which voter turnout for Russia's 1996 presidential election exceeded turnout in the U.S. presidential election that year : 21

Amount by which the number of Americans who watched 1996's Super Bowl exceeded the number who voted in that year's presidential election : 43,000,000

Number of votes cast in an Oklahoma Democratic Senate primary in 1998 for a candidate who had died a month earlier : 56,393

Chance that an American who voted for Ross Perot in 1992 could not recall having done so by 1996 : 1 in 2

Chance that a U.S. member of the Libertarian Party joined within the last five years : 1 in 3

Percentage of Americans who said in 1999 that they would vote for Donald Trump for president over Al Gore or George W. Bush : 5

Percentage who said they would vote for Heather Locklear : 6

The Campaign Trail

Percentage of Americans who believe that politicians don't grant special favors to large campaign contributors : 2

Number of the 106 election-reform bills introduced in the 105th Congress that were passed in both the House and Senate : 0

Rank of the NRA among the organizations that spent the most on House and Senate campaigns during the 1998 election : 2

Number of convicted felons who ran for the position of Chicago alderman in 1995 : 5

Hour at which "voracious criminals go to bed," according to Bob Dole during his last presidential campaign : 6 A.M.

Ratio of legal fees paid by Newt Gingrich's 1996 reelection campaign to the amount it spent on TV and radio ads : 5:4

Amount Bob Dole spent in 1996 on political advertising on the Food Network : $22,000

Estimated points by which the use of negative campaign ads increases the percentage of the vote a national candidate will win : +19

Estimated points by which the use of positive ads will do so : +9

Billions of gallons of water that the GOP reported released into a New Hampshire river in July 1999 for an Al Gore photo op : 4

Billions of gallons actually released, and average amount released into the river each day, respectively : 1.67, 1.9

Percentage of contributions to the Republican National Committee during 1997 and 1998 that were $1,000 or more : 0.24

Percentage of contributions to the Democratic National Committee that were : 1.1

Number of PACs that contributed the legal limit in 1995 to Newt Gingrich's 1996 Georgia primary campaign : 19

Percentage of 1994 congressional campaign contributions made by the top ten corporate PACs that went to Republicans : 45

Percentage that went to Republicans for 1998 campaigns : 67

Amount that the head of Chinese military intelligence gave Clinton fund-raiser Johnny Chung in 1996 : $300,000

Ratio of the amount that Chung spent on himself to the amount he gave to the Democratic National Committee : 14:1

Number of "real ideological differences" within the Democratic party, according to Senator Robert Torricelli in 1998 : 0

Percentage change in the number of labor PACs since 1974 : +58

Percentage change in the number of corporate PACs since then : +1,630

Average percentage change in the GDP in a year preceding a presidential incumbent's reelection since 1950 : +4.1

Average percentage change in the GDP in a year preceding a presidential incumbent's losing reelection : +0.95

Estimated ratio of Steve Forbes's net worth in 1996 to all presidential campaign contributions in the previous year : 5:1

Ratio of campaign spending per vote won by Newt Gingrich in his last campaign to spending per vote won by Senator Russ Feingold that year : 9:1

Ratio of Gingrich's spending per vote in his first successful federal campaign to Feingold's spending per vote in his : 3:1

Percentage of the combined funds in the Senate's five largest campaign chests in 1998 that belonged to Alfonse D'Amato : 37

Number of hands Newt Gingrich shook on August 22, 1997, in an attempt to set the world record for "political handshaking" : 3,609

Percentage of Americans who said in 1997 that they were more likely to see Elvis Presley than campaign-finance reform : 48

Number of years that federal law limited congressional campaign spending before this was ruled unconstitutional in 1976 : 2

Number of Constitutional amendments called for in the 1996 Republican Party platform : 7

Number of times speakers at the 1996 Republican National Convention mentioned Ronald Reagan : 60

Number of times that speakers at the 1996 Democratic National Convention mentioned Newt Gingrich : 114

Percentage of major-party delegates chosen by March 21, 2000 : 70

Percentage who were chosen by March 21 in 1976 : 22

Ratio of major-party presidential primaries held before April in 2000 to those held before April in 1984 : 3:1

Price of *The New Hampshire Primer*, a how-to book on winning the first presidential primary: $9.95

Ratio of Republicans to Democrats elected president since 1900 who lost their bid for reelection : 4:1

Number of the six Senate Republican leaders who ran for president in the twentieth century who won : 0

Minimum amount estimated in 1998 that a major-party presidential candidate would have to raise per hour in 1999 to be nominated : $2,466

Amount raised per hour during the first six months of 1999 by George W. Bush : $8,447

Percentage of eligible Texans who voted for George W. Bush for governor in 1994 and 1998, respectively : 27,22

Last year in which an incumbent Republican governor was elected president : 1896

Number of elected New York City mayors who went on to win higher office in the twentieth century : 0

Days it took Eleanor Roosevelt to decline an invitation to run for U.S. senator from New York in 1945 : 5

The White House

Number of the first five presidents of the United States who died on the fourth of July : 3

Number of U.S. presidents in the twentieth century who left office without having issued a single veto : 0

Number of bills vetoed by Bill Clinton between January 20, 1993, and June 7, 1995 : 0

Number he has vetoed since then : 25

Ratio of Republican to Democrat presidential vetoes over-ridden by Congress since 1960 : 7:1

Number of "difficult, detailed" government-program cuts President Clinton said his 1998 budget contained : 238

Percentage of these that his budget director declared too "boring" to list for reporters at a 1997 press conference : 100

Number of staff engineers and electricians retained by the White House during 1995's government shutdown : 5

Number of Americans who scaled the White House fence between 1989 and 1994 : 22

Percentage of Americans who cited Ronald Reagan as the president who "best personified cool ranch tortilla chips," in a 1995 Snack Food Association poll : 25

Percentage who cited Abraham Lincoln as the president who "best personified pretzel logs" : 37

Chance that a U.S. president was born in a hospital : 1 in 21

Percentage of Americans who said in 1996 that they would rather have Richard Nixon back in the White House than any other president : 3

Percentage of African Americans who said in 1998 that they wished Bill Clinton could run for a third term : 74

Percentage of white Americans who said this : 34

Minimum estimated total public spending on investigations by independent counsels since 1978 : $172,000,000

Ratio of special prosecutors who investigated Richard Nixon to those who have investigated Bill Clinton or his administration : 1:4

Ratio of the amount the special prosecutor's office spent on Watergate to the amount it has spent on Kenneth Starr's investigations of Bill Clinton : 1:2

Chance that an American in 1998 could not name the allegation that Kenneth Starr had already spent three years investigating : 1 in 2

Percentage of days that Bill Clinton spent in the White House in 1998 : 44

Contributions to the Democratic National Committee made between 1994 and 1996 by White House overnight guests, per square foot of the Lincoln bedroom : $14,442.50

Amount that the Paula Jones Legal Fund spent between 1994 and 1997 on "pet care" for a dog named Mitzie : $95

Rank of retired and housewife, among the most common "occupations" of donors to Bill Clinton's legal defense fund through 1998 : 1,2

Number of years that President Clinton's private lawyer David Kendall has vetted articles for the *National Enquirer* : 17

Days after President Clinton was fined $90,000 for lying under oath that he spoke at the American Bar Association's annual meeting in 1999 : 11

Ratio of the number of people indicted by Kenneth Starr since 1994 to the number of whales killed by Captain Ahab in pursuit of Moby Dick : 1:1

Ratio of lines devoted to Hillary Rodham Clinton in the 1999 *Who's Who in America* to those devoted to her husband : 4:1

Percentage of Americans who said in 1996 that they were "more comfortable" with a First Lady who keeps the same hairstyle for an entire term : 17

Percentage of Americans who said in November 1991 that they had not "heard enough" about Bill Clinton : 82

The Congress

Percentage of Americans who believe that senators have "very high ethical standards" : 2

Number of months in 1997 during which Congress imposed a moratorium on hearing new ethics complaints against members : 8

Percentage of Americans who agreed in 1997 that "Congress spends more time complaining about government than running it" : 71

Amount of soft money raised by political parties during the 105th Congress for every campaign-finance-reform bill introduced : $1,662,422

Pages of hearings on campaign finance reform in the U.S. congressional record between 1987 and 1997 : 4,424

Pages of congressional floor speeches on campaign finance reform in the record : 3,675

Length, in pages, of the Senate's 1998 report on the financing of the 1996 Democratic campaigns : 1,112

Number of the report's thirty-three chapters that were devoted to the issue of campaign-finance reform : 1

Portion of her staff that Michigan representative Barbara Collins fired in 1995 for refusing to take a lie-detector test : $\frac{3}{8}$

Chances that a female member of Congress was a Girl Scout : 2 in 3

Percentage of the light switches in Senator Bob Packwood's private Senate quarters that were equipped with dimmers by the time he resigned in 1995 : 100

Weight of evidence brought before the Senate Ethics Committee against Packwood that year, in pounds : 41

Number of nights former congressman Dan Rostenkowski spent at a Salvation Army halfway house in the fall of 1997 : 60

Chance that a witness deposed by a 1991 Senate ethics panel investigating New York Senator Alfonse D'Amato took the Fifth : 1 in 2

Chances that a witness deposed by the Senate's Whitewater committee did : 0

Portion of Senate Gallery seats made available to the public during the 1998 impeachment trial : ⅛

Number of Congress members who attended a March 1998 Capitol Hill hearing on the genocide of Muslims in Bosnia : 4

Number of international treaties pending before the Senate Foreign Relations Committee in September 1999 : 56

Percentage of these that predate the Republican takeover of Congress in 1994 : 57

Increase in the amount of pork in the federal budget since the Republicans took control of Congress in 1994 : $4,400,000,000

Chance that a subpoena issued since 1997 in the House campaign-finance investigation went to a Republican : 1 in 78

Total votes by which Democrats lost six key districts and the chance to regain control of the House in 1998 : 21,898

Number of the fifteen members of the 106th Congress whose net worth exceeds $19 million who are Democrats : 9

Number of legislators who drove foreign cars in Washington last year but used domestic cars at home : 79

Number of parking tickets issued to federal legislators in the District of Columbia in 1998 : 2,652

Ratio of the number of raises Congress has granted itself between 1938 and 2000 to those it has granted minimum-wage workers : 22:19

Chance that a member of Congress who left office in 1994 was a lobbyist by 1996 : 1 in 4

Ratio of the number of House incumbents who ran unopposed in 1998 to the total number of congressmen in 1791 : 1:1

Number of leaks in the Capitol dome : 653

The Courts

Ratio of Americans who can name The Three Stooges to those who can name three Supreme Court justices : 3:1

Estimated number of gun sales prevented by background checks before the Supreme Court made them mandatory in July 1996 : 250,000

Number of questions asked by Justice Clarence Thomas during the 1997 oral arguments of the Paula Jones case : 0

Number of state and federal court opinions written since 1977 that have included a reference to Elvis Presley : 234

Portion of federal judgeships on the Ninth Circuit Court of Appeals that are vacant : ¼

Number of years that at least one fourth of the federal judgeships on the Ninth Circuit Court of Appeals have been vacant : 3

Percentage change between 1995 and 1996 in federal spending on court-appointed attorneys for death-penalty cases : +68

Estimated percentage of all U.S. felony defendants who cannot afford to hire their own lawyer : 85

Months after boxing promoter Don King was acquitted of fraud in 1998 that he took his jurors to the Bahamas : 2

Percentage by which federal funding of legal services for the poor was cut in 1996 : 30

Ratio of federal spending on legal services for the poor in 1999 to spending in 1995 : 3:4

Maximum amount of time that a suspect in Florida can be held in jail without being assigned a lawyer, in hours : 24

Maximum amount of time that a 1999 Texas bill proposed holding suspects before assigning a lawyer, in days : 20

Number of legal-research junkets to foreign countries made by members of Timothy McVeigh's defense team : 9

Number of lawyers, investigators, and technical experts involved in McVeigh's court-appointed defense : 44

Number of interviews conducted with possible witnesses by prosecutors and investigators after the Oklahoma City bombing : 28,000

Number of death sentences upheld by Texas courts during the 1990s for men whose lawyers slept during their trials : 3

Number of U.S. death-row inmates whose sentences have been overturned since 1976 : 78

Number of Philadelphia criminal convictions overturned in 1995 because of police misconduct : 55

Estimated number of the city's police-misconduct cases still pending at the end of that year : 1,200

Percentage of the protesters arrested outside Seattle's World Trade Organization meeting in December 1999 whose charges were dropped due to lack of evidence : 92

Percentage of all second- and third-strike felony convictions in California since 1994 that were for nonviolent offenses : 76

Number of class-action suits that a 1996 law allows the federally funded Legal Services Corporation to represent : 0

Number of suits brought against welfare-reform policies or by prisoners or illegal aliens that the law allows Legal Services to represent : 0

Years it took a prisoner injured in the 1971 Attica Prison riots to win a judgment against New York State : 26

Estimated number of claims by Attica prisoners still pending in 1999 : 1,200

Number of lawsuits for civil-rights violations filed by U.S. prison inmates in 1998 : 13,756

Percentage of lawsuits since 1998 in U.S. courts that result in punitive damages : 0.047

Percentage change since 1987 in the number of expert witnesses listed by the nation's largest referral service : +140

Cost of O. J. Simpson's criminal trial to Los Angeles County, per day of the trial : $50,495

Hours it took a Tennessee jury in December 1999 to decide that the assassination of Martin Luther King was the result of a conspiracy : 2

Crime

Percentage of Americans in 1995 who reported never having been the victim of a violent crime : 86

Number of suburban murder-for-hire cases filed with U.S. law-enforcement agencies between 1988 and 1994 : 1,053

Minimum number of fugitives for whom the FBI has an active warrant : 6,500

Chance that a fatal act of terrorism committed in the U.S. since 1982 was attributed by the FBI to a foreign group : 1 in 3

Ratio of handgun murders per capita in Canada to handgun murders per capita in America in 1996 : 1:324

Percentage change in the homicide rate in Canada since the 1976 abolition of the death penalty there : −49

Chance that a U.S. police chief in 1995 believed the death penalty "significantly reduces the number of homicides" : 1 in 4

Number of serious crimes prevented by every $1 million spent incarcerating repeat felons, according to a 1996 RAND study : 61

Number prevented by every $1 million spent on high-school-graduation incentives : 258

Chance that a U.S. abortion clinic suffered a severely violent attack from protesters in 1998 : 1 in 4

Estimated number of abortions performed on victims of incest or rape each year in the U.S. : 14,000

Estimated number of Catholic priests accused of sexual assault in the U.S. since 1985 : 3,200

Estimated amount U.S. Roman Catholic dioceses have paid to victims of sexual assault since 1985 : $1,000,000,000

Ratio of the number of federal indictments of elected officials in 1974 to the number in 1995 : 1:4

Chance that an American would characterize the President's affair with Monica Lewinsky as "harassment" : 1 in 10

Number of federal fraud charges of which former Mouseketeer Darlene Gillespie was found guilty in 1998 : 9

Number of years before Disney's planned community of Celebration, Florida, experienced its first violent crime : 2

Punishment

Chance that an American born today will spend time in jail : 1 in 20

Number of nonviolent offenders in U.S. prisons in January 2000 : 1,222,155

Rank of New York among states with the highest incidence of wrongful execution between 1900 and 1965 : 1

Number of people sentenced under California's three-strikes law for murder or rape between 1994 and 1997 : 466

Number sentenced for petty theft or drug possession : 11,560

Years in prison to which a California man was sentenced in 1995 after his third burglary offense, the theft of four cookies : 26

Days in jail served by a California man convicted the same year of killing one graffiti vandal and wounding another : 4

Chance that a California adult lives or works in a prison : 1 in 122

Hours of daily operation required of L.A. Central Jail's dry-cleaning machines in 1996 to prepare prisoners' street clothes for storage : 24

Amount the California prison system spent between 1993 and 1998 to prevent birds from being electrocuted by its fences : $3,400,000

Number of nonskid strips the Delaware Correctional Center affixed to its gallows steps before a 1996 hanging : 23

Number of plastic liners with which Florida chain gangs were provided in 1995 to protect them from leg-iron chafing : 280

Tons of rock that Alabama imported in 1995 and 1996 for chain gangs to crush : 188

Minutes after an Oklahoma prisoner was released from the hospital for a drug overdose in 1995 that he was executed : 40

Total settlement paid to three female federal inmates in 1998 after California prison guards sold them as sex slaves to male prisoners : $500,000

Number of the nine prison employees named in the women's lawsuit who were charged with a crime : 0

Amount the city of Albuquerque began charging inmates in 1996 for each night spent in jail : $40

Total amount collected before the program was discontinued after eighteen months : $100,000

Consecutive weeks between 1995 and 1997 that Newt Gingrich's lectures were broadcast in Phoenix jails as part of the sheriff's "get tough" campaign : 156

Years in prison to which a former CIA officer was sentenced in 1998 for trying to extort $1 million from the agency : 5

Year in which he will begin receiving his CIA pension : 2009

Amount of cash inmates compete to grab from between a bull's horns each year at the Oklahoma State Prison Rodeo : $100

Bail set for a Maine man in 1995 after he was arrested for barking at a police dog : $25

SOCIAL STUDIES

The Drug War

The Battle of the Sexes

Black and White

Childhood

Adolescence

Modern Maturity

Traditions

Giving and Receiving

Making It Big

The Drug War

Ratio of Americans who die as a result of illegal-drug use to those who die from smoking-related illnesses each year : 1:21

Number of times since 1906 that Congress has voted against granting the FDA jurisdiction over tobacco : 18

Chance that a U.S. oncologist has recommended marijuana to combat nausea caused by chemotherapy: 1 in 2

Estimated annual amount Americans spend on marijuana, according to the federal government : $7,000,000,000

Minimum annual amount federal, state, and local governments spend combating marijuana, according to NORML : $7,500,000,000

Chance that a first-year U.S. college student favors the legalization of marijuana : 1 in 3

Chances that a first-year U.S. college student believes that courts show "too much concern" for criminals : 3 in 4

Factor by which the number of teenagers using marijuana in 1997 exceeded the number arrested for violent crime : 14

Chances that a drug user holds a full-time job, according to a 1999 federal study : 7 in 10

Months after George W. Bush became a presidential candidate that the study was released : 3

Percentage change in the number of marijuana arrests during the Clinton Administration : +56

Chance that an American sentenced for federal drug convictions in 1991 turned informant in exchange for a reduced sentence : 1 in 5

Percentage of violent offenders in state prisons in 1991 whose crime was committed under the influence of alcohol alone : 21

Percentage whose crime was committed under the influence of crack or cocaine alone : 3

Percentage change since 1991 in the number of U.S. inmates who were illegal-drug users at the time of their arrest : +68

Percentage change since then in the number of such inmates who receive treatment : −32

Chance that a Wyoming inmate under the age of 18 has used crystal meth more than once : 1 in 2

Percentage change since 1995 in the number of heroin overdoses in greater Orlando, Florida : +107

Kilos of heroin found on Colombian President Ernesto Samper's official plane in September 1996 : 8

Factor by which the 123,500 acres of coca that Colombia reported eradicating in 1998 exceeded CIA estimates : 4

Number of Vietnam-era helicopters that the U.S. donated to Mexico for drug control between 1996 and 1997 : 73

Percentage of them that the U.S. agreed to take back in 1998 after Mexico found them defective : 100

Pounds of cocaine that U.S. Customs agents found hidden in the wigs worn by two Jamaican women in August 1999 : 4.02

Estimated portion of the heroin and cocaine used each year in the U.S. that is accounted for by people on bail, probation, or parole : ⅔

Amount of federal funding received last year by Drug Abuse Resistance Education (D.A.R.E.) : $1,750,000

Factor by which D.A.R.E. decreases drug use, according to a study published in the *Journal of Consulting and Clinical Psychology* in 1999 : 0

Percentage change between 1994 and 1997 in Prozac prescriptions or recommendations for children under the age of 12 : +212

Estimated chance that a U.S. boy between the ages of 5 and 14 is on Ritalin : 1 in 20

Ratio of boys to girls on Ritalin : 4:1

Average number of Americans killed each week by prescription drugs : 1,900

Price a Vancouver artist charges for a necklace with a sterling silver pendant cast from an antidepressant pill : $30

Price paid at a Los Angeles auction in 1996 for a drug-rehabilitation discharge signed by Kurt Cobain : $1,150

Number of years that the head of the Partnership for a Drug-Free America served as CEO of a pharmaceutical firm : 12

Factor by which U.S. deaths from prescription and medication errors increased between 1983 and 1996 : 2

Factor by which marijuana use increases the likelihood of other illegal drug use, according to the president of Phoenix House in 1997 : ∞

The Battle of the Sexes

Percentage change in the average amount of cloth required to clothe a U.S. woman between 1913 and 1928 : −64

Number of World War I battleships said to have been built from the steel donated by U.S. women from their corsets : 2

Average amount of food a U.S. woman would have to consume each day in order to eat like a bird, in pounds : 134

Chances that a cartoon in *The New Yorker*'s 1996 Women's Issue was drawn by a man: 5 in 6

Number of the ten WNBA coaching vacancies between June and October 1997 that were filled by men : 7

Change since 1979 in the median earnings of a U.S. woman with a full-time job, in constant dollars : +$3,188

Change since then in the median earnings of a U.S. man with a full-time job : −$2,633

Average amount a man spends on Valentine's Day for every dollar a woman spends : $2.10

Percentage of U.S. men who believe "the country would be better off" if more members of Congress were women : 63

Chance that a portrait of a woman on the Senate side of the Capitol is of Pocahontas : 1 in 2

Chance that a Native American woman was a victim of violence from 1992–96 : 1 in 10

Chance that an African-American woman was : 1 in 18

Number of consecutive years that Colorado state legislators voted down a bill banning female genital mutilation before it passed in 1999 : 3

Percentage of all girls' school facilities in Afghanistan's Taliban territories shut down between 1996 and 1998 : 100

Estimated number of the territories' home-schooling programs for girls shut down in June 1998 : 100

Number of male witnesses that Pakistan requires for a rape prosecution : 4

Estimated chance that a Normal, Illinois, Mitsubishi worker whom the EEOC believes was sexually harassed has ever filed a suit : 1 in 7

Number of calls made in October 1997 to 888-HARASS-U, a hotline set up to report presidential sexual harassment: 4,195

Percentage of Americans earning less than $25,000 a year who believe the President propositioned Paula Jones : 29

Percentage of Americans earning at least $50,000 a year who believe this : 48

Days the President should spend in jail "simply for hitting on a dog like" Paula Jones, according to O. J. Simpson : 30

Days in jail to which a Pennsylvania man was sentenced in 1996 for repeatedly oinking at his ex-wife : 30

Chance that a U.S. woman considers herself a victim of injustice : 1 in 5

Chance that a U.S. man feels that way about himself : 1 in 4

Black and White

Chance that an African American believes that blacks will never obtain equality in the U.S. : 1 in 2

Chance that a black American adult in 1996 preferred being called an "Afro-American" : 1 in 8

Number of U.S. Census respondents in 1990 who identified their race as "other" : 9,804,847

Percentage of them later requestioned by the Census who reported being white : 59

Chance that an African-American man attended the first Million Man March in October 1995 : 1 in 12

Chance that an African-American adult attended Martin Luther King's March on Washington in 1963 : 1 in 60

Chance that an arrest has been made in connection with any of the 163 arson attacks against black southern churches between January 1, 1995 and September 8, 1998 : 1 in 3

Chances that an arrestee was white : 2 in 3

Chances that an arrest has been made in connection with any of the 193 arson attacks made against non-black southern churches during the same period : 2 in 5

Chances that an arrestee was white : 4 in 5

Chance that an American executed since the 1976 reinstatement of the death penalty was a white person who killed an African American : 1 in 50

Chance that a black resident of South Dakota is in prison : 1 in 20

Number of Denny's franchises owned by African Americans in 1993 : 1

Number in 1999 : 123

Percentage of racial epithets published in the *New York Times* in 1995 that consisted of the word "nigger" : 57

Percentage in 1985 : 30

Chance that a New York State resident in 1776 was a slave : 1 in 7

Chance that an African American living in New York State lives below the poverty level : 1 in 4

Average age of the three black professional athletes with the largest incomes in the U.S. in 1998 : 28

Average age of the three white professional athletes with the largest incomes that year : 35

Number of black jockeys who won the Kentucky Derby during its first twenty-eight years : 11

Number who have won it in the ninety-seven years since : 0

Percentage of black teenagers who say it is "extremely important" to learn U.S. history and geography in high school : 59

Percentage of white teenagers who say this : 25

Factor by which the Constitution allowed a state to count its slaves when allocating House seats and electoral votes : ⅗

Votes by which eighteenth-century U.S. lawmakers rejected outlawing slavery in all future states beyond the original thirteen : 1

Estimated number of anti-slavery petitions sent to Congress in 1835 and 1836 : 500

Number of months after the Civil War ended that slaves in Texas were told of their emancipation : 2

Number of years that Texas has observed a "Juneteenth" state holiday to commemorate the day its slaves were told : 19

Year in which Mississippi ratified the Thirteenth Amendment to the U.S. Constitution, abolishing slavery : 1995

Year in which the Tennessee legislature approved the Fifteenth Amendment, granting blacks the right to vote : 1997

Rank of Strom Thurmond's 1957 filibuster against civil rights legislation among the longest filibusters in U.S. history : 1

Chance that a work of art on display in the Capitol includes a depiction of an African American : 1 in 70

Percentage change between 1992 and 1996 in the number of African-American delegates at the Republican National Convention : −51

Percentage of white Americans who said in 1997 that they would vote for Colin Powell over Al Gore for president in 2000 : 53

Percentage of non-white Americans who said this : 34

Percentage of Supreme Court decisions on which justices Clarence Thomas and Antonin Scalia have agreed : 88

Percentage change in the number of black students admitted to Berkeley Law School since California banned affirmative action in 1997 : −58

Number of the fourteen black students that the school admitted in 1997 who decided to attend : 0

Number of states in 1990 in which a black college graduate's average income was at least 90 percent of a white college graduate's : 4

Percentage of white Americans in 1995 who believed their race had hindered their ability to achieve the American dream : 11

Childhood

Chances that a person directly affected by the 1996 welfare-reform law was old enough to vote : 2 in 5

Percentage change since 1989 in the number of children living in poverty who have at least one working parent : +30

Percentage of U.S. children who say their greatest wish for their parents is that they make more money : 23

Percentage who say their greatest wish for their parents is that they "spend more time with me" : 11

Percentage of U.S. children of divorce in 1991 who had not seen their father in at least a year : 40

Number of states sued in federal court in 1998 for inadequate care of foster children : 20

Average number of Americans under the age of 18 killed by their parents or caretakers each day : 5

Ratio of children's emergency-room visits for injuries related to fireworks in 1992 to those related to "desk supplies" : 1:5

Ratio in 1997, after the Consumer Product Safety Commission stopped classifying pens and pencils as "desk supplies" : 3:2

Number of children treated for sledding injuries in 1998 : 46,067

Chance that a U.S. child will be diagnosed with cancer before the age of ten : 1 in 667

Gallons of peppermint-flavored liquid Prozac prescribed in 1997 : 27,012

Rank of Catwoman among the "superheroes" that U.S. boys under the age of ten reported most wanting to be in 1997 : 1

Amount raised by a Denver fourth-grade class since 1998 in a campaign to help Christian Solidarity International buy and free Sudanese slaves : $60,000

Estimated number of slaves "redeemed" as a result : 480

Number of "Your Own Business" patches sold by Girl Scouts of the U.S.A. since 1997 : 3,731

Number of days before winning the 1996 U.S. Figure Skating Championship that Tara Lipinski lost a baby tooth : 5

Percentage change between 1995 and 1996 in the average tooth-fairy payment, per tooth : +10

Average weekly allowance for a U.S. child : $5.82

Average number of murders a U.S. child sees on television before completing elementary school : 8,000

Percentage change in the number of network evening news stories on homicide since 1990 : +474

Average amount spent on direct advertising to U.S. children in 1983, per child : $2.68

Average amount in 1998 : $36.60

Rank of the Budweiser frog TV-ad campaign, among the most popular commercials with children over the age of six in 1998 : 1

Adolescence

Chance that a U.S. parent believes that teenagers are usually "lively and fun to be around" : 1 in 4

Chance that the bedroom of a U.S. child between the ages of ten and sixteen contains a TV set : 1 in 2

Percentage of U.S. teenagers who believe "TV shows should help teach kids right from wrong" : 82

Number of America's twenty largest cities that impose a night-time curfew on minors : 19

Portion of the seventy American juvenile offenders on death row who are in Texas : ⅓

Estimated percentage of U.S. counties in which no homicides were committed by juveniles in 1997 : 88

Percentage in which at least two were : 7

Chance that an adolescent U.S. boy has been intentionally hit or kicked in the genitals : 1 in 10

Chances that the perpetrator was a girl : 2 in 5

Average number of performance days lost per U.S. high-school cheerleading injury each year : 28.8

Average number lost per high-school football injury : 5.6

Rank of self-inflicted wounds among the top injuries for which teenage girls over the age of fifteen were hospitalized in New York State in 1998 : 1

Rank of assault among the top reasons that teenage boys over the age of 15 were hospitalized that year : 1

Change since 1977 in the percentage of white American high school seniors who smoke : −0.6

Change since then in the percentage of African-American high school seniors who do : −17.5

Points by which the percentage of white U.S. teenage girls who say they are dissatisfied with their bodies exceeds the percentage of African-American girls who say this : 60

Percentage of U.S. teenagers who say they have dated someone of a different race : 47

Chance that a U.S. teenage girl will become pregnant within one month of becoming sexually active : 1 in 5

Modern Maturity

Average number of Americans who turn fifty each day : 10,065

Chance that a member of the American Association of Retired Persons holds a paying job : 1 in 3

Ratio of the amount the federal government spent in 1995 on Americans under eighteen to the amount it spent on those over sixty-five : 1:5

Ratio of reporters who attended the lift-off of John Glenn's first space flight in 1962 to those who covered his 1998 shuttle flight : 1:7

Chance that an ad in the January 1996 issue of *Esquire* offered products or services relating to hair loss : 1 in 4

Percentage of Americans over the age of sixty-five who say color is a "very important" factor in buying underwear : 30

Number of years Nazi filmmaker Leni Riefenstahl has been a member of Greenpeace : 8

Estimated number of former Nazi SS officers or their dependents who received pension payments from the German government in 1996 : 65,000

Number of them living in the U.S. at the time : 3,377

Percentage of Dan Rostenkowski's congressional pension benefits he forfeited during his stay in prison in 1996 : 0

Percentage change since 1989 in the number of federal prison inmates over the age of forty-nine : +110

Chance that an inmate over the age of fifty-five has been incarcerated for less than a year : 1 in 4

Chance that a California nursing home was cited for violations "causing death or life-threatening harm" to patients between 1997 and 1998 : 1 in 3

Average number of neuro-active drugs Timothy Leary ingested each day during the last year of his life, according to his Web site : 8

Average number of different drug prescriptions filled each year by an American over the age of seventy-four : 12

Chance that a cancer patient over the age of eighty-five living in a nursing home does not receive adequate pain medication : 1 in 3

Rank of adults over seventy among the age groups most in favor of making cigarettes illegal : 1

Rank of the elderly among age groups most likely to believe in 1996 that Bob Dole's age would make him a "less able" president : 1

Year in which Barbara Bush was named "First Lady of the Century" by *Outlaw Biker* magazine : 1995

Age at which Elizabeth Dole became a Republican : 39

Estimated number of U.S. senior citizens who played tackle football last year : 224,000

Number of Americans who are at least one hundred years old : 62,000

Traditions

Percentage of British fluid intake that is tea : 42

Number of people injured during a 1995 cheese-rolling competition held in Cheltenham, England : 18

Number of reasons to hate the French published by London's *Daily Star* in 1999 after France refused to lift its ban on British beef : 21

Percentage change since 1995 in the number of the world's surgeons who cleanse wounds with maggots : +400

Number of the forty-four U.S. House and Senate committees chaired by white men in 1995 : 41

Number today : 43

Last year in which neither a Dole nor a Bush has appeared on the Republican presidential ticket : 1972

Number of years that the mother in the "Family Circus" cartoon wore the same hairstyle before it was changed in 1995 : 36

Weight in pounds of Thailand's 1999 Jumbo Queen, displaying "the grace, elegance, and enormity of an elephant" : 352

Length in feet of a wooden penis carried through the streets of Komaki, Japan, during its annual spring fertility ceremony : 8.3

Number of years Bryn Mawr College has held an annual Mayhole Celebration, "a feminist takeoff on the maypole" : 14

Minimum number of U.S. Army bases in which space has been reserved for Wiccan soldiers' seasonal rites : 8

Number of U.S. military service medals that cannot be purchased without an authorized signature : 1

Percentage of Boy Scout merit badges whose purchase requires a signature: 100

Number of fishing rods and tackle boxes that can be checked out of Georgia's Tybee Island public library : 25

Price of a set of How to Build Your Own Casket instructions, from Alameda Cremations of California : $9.95

Estimated number of angels that can dance on the head of a pin, according to the American Institute of Physics : 10^{64}

Estimated number that can dance in a row across a pinhead's diameter, "Rockettes-style" : 10^{32}

Giving and Receiving

Average percentage of all gold refined worldwide since 1990 that was made into jewelry : 79

Price of an anatomically correct, one-pound chocolate replica of a human heart, from the Anatomical Chart and Model Catalog : $24.90

Estimated number of candy hearts that the New England Confectionary Company made in 1998 : 8,000,000,000

Estimated number that said, "Fax Me" : 1,800,000

Estimated average number of donations received each week through the ATM in the lobby of North Carolina's Unity Center of Peace Church : 7

Donation received in 1998 by a Los Angeles soup kitchen in order to provide new shopping carts to the homeless : $10,000

Estimated number of serfs Catherine the Great gave away as gifts in the eighteenth century : 45,000

Estimated number of copies of *Winnie the Pooh* Argentina's foreign minister gave to residents of the Falkland Islands for Christmas in 1998 : 175

Estimated percentage of the drugs donated to victims of the Bosnian war between 1992 and 1998 that were unusable : 50

Factor by which combined U.S. individual charitable donations in 1998 exceeded those of foundations and corporations : 5.7

Percentage of proceeds of a 1998 AIDS fund-raising bike ride across Texas that was used to cover production costs : 85

Number of radio stations that offered Chelsea Clinton a car for her sixteenth birthday : 3

Amount Disney spent in 1995 to outfit Tipper and Al Gore as Beauty and the Beast for Halloween : $8,365

Percentage of this amount for which Disney was reimbursed by the Democratic National Committee : 100

Minimum campaign contribution that White House tapes released in 1997 reveal President Richard Nixon citing as the price of an ambassadorship : $250,000

Weight in pounds of a bronze elephant donated to the U.N. in 1998 by Kenya, Namibia, and Nepal : 7,000

Number of days before its unveiling that potted plants were positioned to obscure its penis : 1

Number of the 535 free subscriptions *Hustler* offered members of Congress in 1997 that were rejected : 16

Percentage by which Congress proposed in 1999 to cut non-defense discretionary spending in 2002 : 18

Percentage by which non-defense discretionary spending had increased in the previous decade : 18

Estimated number of jokes donated to the Library of Congress in 1998 by Bob Hope : 1,000,000

Estimated amount Studs Terkel gave a burglar who broke into his Chicago home in 1998 : $280

Amount the burglar returned when Terkel said to him, "Hey, I'm flat broke now. How about twenty bucks to tide me over 'til tomorrow?" : $20

Making It Big

Estimated number of "well-documented" sightings of Bigfoot since 1958 : 1,500

Number of Squadron Supreme comic books printed in 1997 with ink containing its creator's ashes : 4,000

Amount Richard Nixon's estate is seeking from the U.S. government for documents the government seized after Nixon left office : $210,000,000

Speaking fees earned in 1996 by *Book of Virtues* author and former Secretary of Education William Bennett : $1,800,000

Speed at which an Iowa state trooper clocked a car last July in which Pat Buchanan was on the phone with Oliver North, in miles per hour : 66

Price of the ticket that North, via cell phone, charmed the trooper out of writing : $54

Price paid at auction in 1996 for a 1975 Ford Escort previously owned by Pope John Paul II : $102,000

Number of times CBS's 1999 press release for *Jesus*, the miniseries, mentions the "billions" of Christians He inspired : 2

Number of times it mentions or implies that He was Jewish : 0

Percentage change since 1983 in the number of miracles required to become a saint : −50

Ratio of the median U.S. waiting period for a human liver transplant in 1995 to the amount of time Mickey Mantle waited before receiving one that year : 8:3

Number of specials named after O. J. Simpson trial participants on the menu of the Mo' Better Meaty Meat Burger restaurant in Los Angeles in 1996 : 4

Weeks after Frank Gifford's adultery became public in 1997 that his approval rating had exceeded that of Newt Gingrich by eight points : 3

Federal funds spent in 1996 and 1997 to gild Gingrich's office ceiling, gold excluded : $40,400

Number of Congress members in 1996 who were openly gay : 4

Number of Hollywood's one hundred top-grossing actors that year who were : 0

Number of months Jack Ryan, a designer of the first Barbie Doll, was married to Zsa Zsa Gabor : 9

Number of missiles Ryan designed for the Pentagon : 2

Number of months former congresswoman Pat Schroeder was a contributing editor of Glamour : 12

Year in which Gerald Ford modeled for the cover of Cosmopolitan : 1942

Year in which Marie Antoinette convinced France's King Louis XVI to declare that all handkerchiefs be square : 1785

Ratio of Playboy Playmates who "most admire" Albert Einstein to those who claim to feel this way about Sammy Davis Jr. : 5:13

Years after producing Howard Stern's TV show that Dan Forman became executive news producer at NBC's New York affiliate : 1

Years after John Wayne Gacy became an Illinois Democratic Party precinct captain that he was arrested for 33 murders : 3

Price a Gacy Web site charges for a color photocopy of a 1976 photograph of Gacy with Rosalyn Carter : $15

Ratio of the market value of Bob Dole's signature to that of Unabomber Ted Kaczynski : 1:50

Number of marriage proposals received by Oklahoma City bomber Timothy McVeigh in the three months following his 1995 arrest : 4

Rank of Oprah Winfrey among the celebrities Americans believed most qualified for the U.S. presidency in 1995 : 1

Rank of meeting the Spice Girls among the "greatest moments of my life" according to Prince Charles in 1998 : 1

Tons of flowers and other tokens deposited outside Princess Diana's palace in the week following her death : 11,200

Price paid at auction in 1995 for a diamond-monogrammed gold shoehorn belonging to Frank Sinatra : $5,520

Factor by which Sinatra's birth weight in 1915 exceeds the average weight of a baby born in New Jersey today : 2

HISTORY

The Cold War

Winners and Losers

Arms and Armaments

Military Personnel

The Course of Empire

Diplomacy

Secrets

Déjà Vu

The Cold War

Number of La-Z-Boy recliners delivered to the CIA in January 1996 : 50

Ratio of annual U.S. defense spending to the combined annual defense spending of Russia, China, North Korea, Iran, Iraq, and Libya : 2.3:1

Year in which the U.S. promised the U.S.S.R. that NATO would not expand : 1990

Year that it expanded : 1997

Estimated number of land mines removed and demolished worldwide in 1995 : 100,000

Estimated number of new mines laid that year : 2,000,000

Ratio of the number of doctors on active duty for the Pentagon to the estimated number required during wartime : 4:3

Average amount the Pentagon has spent each day since 1995 to maintain its grounds : $1,613

Amount the Pentagon spent in 1996 to equip Andrews Air Force Base with a third golf course : $7,000,000

Expenditures for which the Pentagon could not account in 1998 : $22,000,000,000

Change in the number of Trident II warheads in the U.S. nuclear arsenal between 1990 and 1998 : +1,152

Average number of U.S. cruise missiles launched per month during the Clinton Administration : 11

Ratio of the 1999 federal budget to the average annual federal budget during World War II, in 1999 dollars : 2:1

Ratio of "major" U.S. Army deployments abroad between 1946 and 1989 to those between 1990 and 1999 : 2:3

Percentage change in the combined budgets of Radio Free Europe and Radio Liberty since the fall of the Berlin Wall in 1989 : –56

Ratio of the number of times since 1993 that Russia's GDP was lower than the previous year's to the number of times Cuba's was : 5:4

Percentage change between 1995 and 1996 in the GDPs of Russia and Cuba, respectively : –5, +8

Rank of getting "rid of" Fidel Castro among the top foreign-policy priorities announced by Senator Phil Gramm in the 1996 presidential campaign : 1

Rank of the U.S. delegation among the largest foreign groups attending the World Festival of Youth and Students in Cuba in 1997 : 1

Portion of U.N. peacekeeping missions ever undertaken that have occurred since the end of the Cold War : ½

Average annual amount the U.S. spent on nuclear-arms programs during the Cold War : $3,700,000,000

Average annual amount that the Department of Energy will spend on nuclear-arms programs through the year 2008 : $4,500,000,000

Tons of uranium from Russia's nuclear arsenal that the country plans to sell to a U.S. company over the next twenty years : 500

Years after Nikita Khrushchev said that Richard Nixon's grand-children would live in a Communist America that his son Sergei took the U.S. citizenship test : 42

Winners and Losers

Ratio of Illinois death-row inmates executed since 1976 to the number declared innocent : 1:1

Rank of God among those publicly thanked by defense lawyer Johnnie Cochran after the O. J. Simpson verdict was delivered in 1995 : 1

Change between 1994 and 1995 in the membership of the Christian Coalition : −43,407

Number of popes stabbed, strangled, or poisoned to death in the last three decades of the tenth century : 5

Percentage of the 14,000 Bulgar survivors of the 1014 battle at Kleidion who were blinded by the victorious Byzantines : 99

Rank of "shed[ding] my enemies' blood and wring[ing] tears from their women" among Genghis Khan's greatest joys : 1

Rank of "crush[ing] your enemies . . . and hear[ing] the lamen-tations of women" among Conan the Barbarian's : 1

Days of imprisonment and torture undergone by Niccolò Machiavelli after falling out of favor with the Medicis in 1513 : 28

Number of years later that his book *The Prince* was published, with a dedication to Lorenzo de' Medici : 9

Months after the publication of Newt Gingrich's 1995 book *To Renew America* that his publisher asked retailers to cut the price by 38 percent : 6

Number of the twenty-three mentions of the word "Newtonian" in the *New York Times* in 1995 that referred to the ideas of Isaac Newton : 10

Year by which Dan Quayle said in 1998 that he was convinced that Republicans would "select a nominee that will beat Bill Clinton" : 2000

Rank of the Prohibition Party among U.S. third parties to have nominated a candidate in the largest number of consecutive presidential elections : 1

Ratio of the amount J. P. Morgan spent on cigars in 1863 to the amount he paid a man to fight in his place in the Civil War : 1:1

Percentage by which the breakup of Standard Oil increased the size of John D. Rockefeller's personal wealth : 200

Price of a bottle of Czar Nicholas II's champagne salvaged in 1998 from a ship sunk in 1916 : $4,922

Number of bids received by the Russian government in 1998 when it put one of its oil companies up for sale : 0

Number of bids received after the asking price was reduced by 25 percent a month later : 0

Years it took Russia to win its armed conflict with the Chechens during the nineteenth century : 47

Number of days it took the German army to conquer Yugoslavia in World War II's "Operation Punishment" : 11

Number of slave laborers that Volkswagen admits to having used in one of its factories during World War II : 17,000

Number of German companies negotiating slave-labor settlements with survivors' groups and the U.S. State Department in 1999 : 16

Estimated chance that a veteran admitted to a VA hospital is homeless : 1 in 4

Rank of the VA, among the country's largest employers of social workers : 1

Ratio of aerospace jobs lost in California since 1995 to the number of new jobs in the film industry : 3:50

Projected gross civilian job losses that will result from scheduled military base closures between 1988 and 1999 : 135,259

Number of civilian jobs created on former military bases in the first eleven years of base closures since then : 49,075

Subsidies for Dungeness crab fishermen included in Congress's emergency appropriations for the 1999 bombing of Yugoslavia : $3,000,000

Average change in a Democratic president's approval rating after sending troops into a new conflict, in percentage points : +0.5

Average change in a Republican president's approval rating : +5

Days after President Franklin Roosevelt's death in April 1945 that Harry Truman was informed of the existence of the atomic bomb : 13

Price paid at auction in 1998 for two landscape watercolors and a line drawing by Adolf Hitler : $80,000

Amount by which the pre-auction estimate of the work's value exceeded this : $67,500

Price paid at a charity auction in 1995 for a turtleneck worn by Jimmy Carter during cease-fire talks in the Bosnian conflict : $5,000

Ratio of the number of sorties U.S. planes flew over Iraq in 1999 to the number they flew over Yugoslavia in the NATO campaign in April that year : 1:1.8

Percentage of Americans who said they were not sure whether the U.S. or Slobodan Milosevic won the war in Kosovo sixteen days after it was over : 40

Chance that a U.S. adult cannot name any country against which the U.S. fought during World War II : 1 in 3

Arms and Armaments

Percentage of worldwide weapons exports in 1997 sold by the five countries on the U.N. Security Council : 86

Percentage sold by the U.S. : 44

Portion of all U.S. arms sales abroad between 1993 and 1997 that were brokered by the Pentagon : ½

Number of full-time federal employees assigned to handle foreign arms sales : 6,300

Annual federal spending on promotional activities for U.S. arms dealers : $444,200,000

Number of years the U.S. Army estimates its supply of aircraft-size camouflage coverings will last : 159

Value of surplus weapons and equipment a Georgia Air Force base lost track of between 1991 and 1994 : $39,000,000

Number of the four 500-pound bombs aboard an Air Force jet lost in the Colorado Rockies in 1997 that have been found : 0

Estimated number of Cobra attack helicopters privately owned by Americans : 25

Pounds of armor worn by a European knight in the eleventh and thirteenth centuries, respectively : 71, 90

Chances that one of the forty-nine armed conflicts fought worldwide since 1990 relied exclusively on small arms : 9 in 10

Maximum range at which China North Industries' "portable laser disturber" can "injure or dizzy the eyes," in miles : 6

Estimated number of firebomb-wielding live bats that the U.S. considered dropping on Japan in early 1944 : 1,000,000

Percentage of Americans in 1995 who didn't know that Hiroshima was the site of the first atomic-bomb attack : 35

Percentage who believed the attack was ordered by Richard Nixon : 1

Amount by which the ten-year defense budget proposed by Bill Clinton in the fall of 1999 exceeded that of House Democrats : $158,000,000

Amount by which it exceeded that of House Republicans : $206,000,000

Number of Tomahawk cruise missiles the U.S. could launch for the price of the Whitewater investigation : 40

Funding that Congress allocated in the 1999 federal budget for military programs not requested by the Pentagon : $1,229,000,000

Amount Senator Trent Lott asked the Senate to allocate for the construction of a battleship in his home state of Mississippi in 1999 : $500,000,000

Amount the U.S. Navy reported that construction would cost : $295,000,000

Factor by which the B-52 stealth bomber's maintenance hours in 1998 exceeded its flight hours that year : 24.6

Ratio of the cost of building an F-22 fighter jet to that of upgrading an F-15 to twice the F-22's effectiveness : 1,500:1

Number of consecutive intercept tests failed by the Army's $15.8-billion high-altitude anti-missile system between 1995 and 1999 : 6

Years behind schedule the system's research-and-development program is running : 3.75

Total number of nuclear weapons worldwide when the first nuclear test ban negotiations began in 1958 : 10,713

Percentage by which the number had changed by the signing of the Limited Test Ban Treaty in 1963 : +220

Number of false alarms of nuclear missile attacks generated by the U.S. early warning system between 1977 and 1984 : 20,784

Number of U.S. nuclear bombs currently on "high alert" : 2,380

Chance that an American favors the resumption of any form of nuclear-weapons testing : 1 in 10

Chance that the leader of a NATO member country in 1999 was once an antiwar or antinuclear activist : 1 in 3

Military Personnel

Chance that a soldier who died in combat in a twentieth-century war was American : 1 in 72

Chance that a civilian who died in a twentieth-century war was American : 1 in 62,000

Number of survivors of Spanish-American War soldiers who received Veterans Department benefits in 1999 : 879

Years it took the Japanese government to apologize for using South Korean POWs as "comfort women" for its troops : 51

Estimated number of South Koreans officially registered in 1995 as "club women" for U.S. military bases : 18,000

Estimated ratio of veterans reporting Gulf War Syndrome symptoms to total U.S. Vietnam War combat deaths : 4:1

Number of Vietnamese in Vietnam in 1969, per U.S. soldier stationed there : 30

Number of Chechens in Chechnya in 1995, per Russian soldier stationed there : 77

Pounds of gold jewelry and dental fillings amassed during wartime by a single SS officer : 1,637

Number of soldiers and veterans testifying at Timothy McVeigh's 1997 bombing trial who claimed he was a model soldier : 11

Months after a child molester was paroled from prison in 1994 that a VA hospital gave him a penile implant : 10

Maximum amount the Canadian government has agreed to spend on a soldier's sex-change operation in U.S. dollars : $13,500

Average amount the U.S. military spent in 1997 on recruiting, per soldier enlisted : $7,187

Average amount spent in 1989 : $5,562

Estimated amount the Pentagon spent during the 1980s to replace the homosexuals it discharged : $471,146,000

Percentage decrease in the number of U.S. Army troops since 1989 : 40

Number of U.S. generals prosecuted for adultery since 1951 : 0

Number of U.S. military personnel convicted of adultery in 1996 : 124

Estimated percentage change since 1997 in the number of Air Force pilots who have voluntarily left the service : +66

Percentage change in the annual number of lesbians and gay men discharged from the U.S. armed forces since 1994 : +86

Percentage change since 1993 in the Pentagon's recruitment advertising budget : +109

Estimated amount the Pentagon will spend through 2001 on U.S. military base closures begun in 1988 : $23,000,000,000

Estimated amount the Pentagon expects to save by base closures through 2001 : $14,000,000,000

Number of dairy cows maintained by the U.S. Naval Academy in 1996 : 350

Amount by which the Naval Academy's cost of producing a gallon of milk that year exceeded the average wholesale price : 30¢

Circumference in inches of the biceps of the G.I. Joe Extreme doll introduced in 1998, if he were six feet tall : 27.3

The Course of Empire

Number of countries to which the U.S. has officially deployed combat ground troops since 1950 : 21

Portion of them in which U.S. troops are still stationed : ½

Number of countries that have received U.S. military aid since 1995 in preparation for NATO expansion : 19

Value of international defense loans the U.S. has written off since 1990 : $10,000,000,000

Factor by which the Congressional Budget Office's 1997 estimate of the U.S. cost of NATO expansion over the next decade exceeded the Pentagon's estimate : 6.8

Year in which General Dwight Eisenhower said that NATO "will have failed" if U.S. troops were in Europe a decade later : 1951

Number of years that Chinese officials reassured Hong Kong residents that "dancing will continue" there after the 1997 takeover : 50

Chance that a Hong Kong resident reported being "very worried" in 1997 about the loss of personal freedom under Chinese rule : 1 in 20

Chance that a Hong Kong resident reported being "very worried" about increased corruption : 1 in 6

Minimum number of Geneva Convention violations of which NATO was accused following its 1999 bombings of Serbia : 18

Estimated percentage change since 1500 in the size of the Native-American population in the territory that became Canada : +22

Estimated percentage change since then in the size of the Native-American population in the territory that became the U.S. : −76

Number of U.S. high school students enrolled in Latin classes in 1962 : 700,000

Number in 1999 : 215,000

Estimated chance that a person living in Italy during the country's 1861 unification spoke Italian : 1 in 40

Estimated chance that a person living in France during the French Revolution spoke French : 1 in 2

Percentage of the French government's 1788 expenditures that went to support the court at Versailles : 6

Percentage that went to finance war debt resulting from the country's support of the colonies in the American Revolution : 50

Chances that a Briton believes that England did more harm than good to its colonies : 3 in 5

Acres of English farmland purchased by the Mormon Church since 1993 : 13,500

Number of years the British Virgin Islands have banned "Rastafarians and hippies" from entering the territory : 20

Number of days in 1998 that a teen was suspended from Georgia's Greenbrier High School after wearing a Pepsi shirt on the school's "Coke Day" : 1

Rank of Philip Morris, among the largest U.S. investors in Poland in 1996 : 1

Number of wars fought before 1999 between countries that both had at least one McDonald's franchise : 0

Diplomacy

Days after China's 1999 announcement that it would begin acquiring offensive weapons that it was accepted into the World Trade Organization : 7

Ratio of human-rights declarations signed by China to those signed by the U.S. : 6:5

Percentage change between 1995 and 1997 in the number of China's U.S. Embassy staffers assigned to congressional relations : +100

Number of Chinese dissidents "known to be active" at the end of 1996, according to the State Department : 0

Value of Pentagon-brokered U.S. arms sales to Taiwan in 1998, expressed as a percentage of Pentagon-brokered sales to Israel : 92

Rank of China among the least effective lobbyists in Washington, according to U.S. Ambassador Jim Sasser in 1997 : 1

Chances that a country to which the U.S. sells arms is cited by Amnesty International for torturing its citizens : 2 in 3

Number of countries besides Australia that have ever formally recognized Indonesia's sovereignty over East Timor : 0

Number of Turkish troops that crossed the Iraqi border in May 1997 to attack Kurds : 25,000

Number of the ten largest U.S. newspapers that gave the story front-page coverage : 0

Months after a Hard Rock Cafe opened in Beirut in 1996 that the U.S. lifted its ban on travel in Lebanon : 7

Amount Cambodia agreed to pay a U.S. lobbying firm in 1999 to "recast" Hun Sen's government "in a favorable light" : $550,000

Head of cattle that Hyundai's founder brought from South Korea on a 1998 visit to North Korea's Kim Jung Il : 1,000

Amount Shell Oil paid in 1999 to sponsor the wedding reception of the King of Buganda, Uganda : $3,000

Number of times the musical *Evita* has been performed in Argentina : 0

Number of times reporters broke into laughter during a 1995 White House press briefing on Bosnia : 5

Ratio of visits to Bosnia, Kosovo, or Albania made by President Clinton since 1992 to those made by the editor of *Soldier of Fortune* : 3:7

Number of hours a Moscow hotel flew a Microsoft flag within view of Red Square during Bill Gates's first visit in November 1997 : 36

Number of lunches Gates ate in Moscow that were not from McDonald's : 0

Number of Ben & Jerry's Peace Pops sold each week through Pentagon vending machines : 12

Years from now, "in a perfect world," that no tobacco manufacturers would exist, according to the Liggett Group's CEO on *The Charlie Rose Show* in 1997 : 30

Secrets

Portion of all pages of CIA documents scheduled to be declassified by 2003 that the agency considers exempt : ⅔

Estimated percentage of CIA documents regarding Iran's 1953 coup that the agency has destroyed : 95

Number of years of legal action it took to get the CIA to release the annual U.S. intelligence budget in October 1997 : 30

Average amount the U.S. spent on intelligence each day in 1996 : $72,876,712

Weeks after Russian president Boris Yeltsin had a heart attack in June 1996 that the CIA found out about it : 11

Estimated number of news stories published worldwide on India's nuclear-bomb capabilities in the four months preceding its 1998 bomb test : 500

Number of CIA analysts who predicted that the test would occur : 0

Year in which some of the nuclear "secrets" that Congress alleged in 1999 that China stole were published in the U.S. : 1984

Hours it took two men to win a 1998 contest to decode the federal government's data-scrambling system : 56

Number of CIA laptops containing top-secret information that were sold inadvertently at a government-surplus auction in 1995 : 25

Pages of the British royal family's medical records found in a folder lying by the side of a Scottish road in 1999 : 70

Pages of the Watergate special prosecutor's report that have been released to the public : 0

Ratio of hours of Nixon White House tapes released since 1974 to hours yet to be released : 1:8

Number of independent-prosecutor cases since 1987 in which targets, allegations, and prosecutors have not been made public : 2

Number of witnesses called since 1997 in the House campaign-finance investigation who have taken the Fifth : 53

Number of federal wiretap warrants granted for criminal investigations in 1996 : 581

Number granted that year for espionage investigations by the U.S. Foreign Intelligence Surveillance Court : 839

Estimated amount U.S. intelligence agencies spent on psychics between 1972 and 1995 : $20,000,000

Estimated number of times that the late former congresswoman Clare Boothe Luce dropped acid : 12

Number of years that Julia Child was employed by a U.S. intelligence agency : 3

Year in which George Bush attended a CIA intelligence meeting wearing a red wig and false nose : 1975

Déjà Vu

Year in which a U.S. secretary of state first advocated the annexation of Cuba : 1823

Last year in which America had as bad a relationship with Britain as it did in 1996, according to former Secretary of State James Baker that year : 1773

Year in which the British sacked the city of Washington and burned the White House : 1814

Amount by which the Beatles outearned the Rolling Stones in 1994 : $9,000,000

Number of California driver's licenses made out to Jesus Christ in 1995 : 123

Number made out to Jesus Christ II : 1

Percentage of Americans who said in 1999 that they believe the new millennium will likely "bring the second coming of Jesus Christ" : 26

Number of times Elizabeth Dole mentioned Ronald Reagan in her endorsement of George W. Bush for president in 2000 : 5

Highest bid offered at auction in May 1997 for the Watergate Hotel lock that was taped in 1972 to get into DNC offices : $13,000

Bid the seller expected : $20,000

Number of spare parts that NASA retrieved from an Alabama museum in 1999 to use on a space shuttle : 2

Federal funds spent on maintaining nuclear testing facilities since U.S. testing was halted in 1992 : $2,224,180,000

Year in which Congress banned the State Department's military training program for Indonesian troops : 1992

Number of years after this that the Pentagon's military training program for Indonesian troops continued : 6

Estimated number of corruption charges filed against Imelda Marcos by the Filipino government in the late 1980s that are still pending : 316

Estimated number added since then, also pending : 100

Number of days after escaping a Danish prison in August 1995 that an inmate asked to be allowed back in : 26

Estimated attendance at Jesse James's third burial, held in Kearney, Missouri, in October 1995 : 550

Number of coffins unearthed by floods in North Carolina in September 1999 : 110

Chances that a U.S. woman whose cosmetic breast implants were removed in 1996 had them replaced the same year : 2 in 3

GEOGRAPHY

State of the World

Africa

Asia

Russia

The Middle East

Europe

Latin America and the Caribbean

Migration

Transportation

American Pie

New York, New York

Going South

State of the World

Percentage of the world's land that was claimed by centralized, sovereign governments in 1500 : 21

Percentage today : 91

Rank of arms trading, illegal drug trafficking, and oil production among the world's largest industries : 1,2,3

Number of countries whose 1996 GDP was less than worldwide spending at Wal-Mart that year : 161

Portion of the world's population whose countries are under U.S. economic sanctions : ½

Chances that a dollar of American foreign aid is spent in the U.S. : 4 in 5

Number of the world's twenty largest banks that are European or Japanese, respectively : 11, 8

Number that are American : 1

Amount the World Bank finished spending in 1997 on an expansion of its Washington headquarters : $314,000,000

Amount by which this exceeded the original budget : $103,000,000

Amount the Bank spent to gild its headquarters' ceilings : $400,000

Number of institutions that are on a "higher moral ground" than the World Bank, according to its president in 1998 : 0

Chance that a human being lives in the U.S. : 1 in 20

Chance that a human being living in a prison does : 1 in 4

Factor by which the U.S. incarceration rate exceeds that of China : 2.5

Chance that a U.N. peacekeeper deployed in 1994 was an American : 1 in 77

Chance that one deployed from July 1998 to June 1999 was : 1 in 31

Chance that a U.N. peacekeeper on duty in 1998 came from a G-7 country : 1 in 6

Ratio of non-Americans to Americans killed in U.S.-embassy bombings between 1983 and 1998 : 10:1

Ratio of civilian U.N. workers killed in the line of duty in 1999 to soldiers killed in U.N. peacekeeping operations : 4:3

Number of people killed worldwide by pirates in 1998 : 78

Estimated ratio of the number of U.N. employees to the number of CIA employees, worldwide : 1:2

Percentage change between 1973 and 1995 in the number of full-time photographers employed by *National Geographic* : −87

Percentage change since then: +250

Chance that a job in one of the ten largest industrialized countries is industrial : 1 in 5

Ratio of hospitals to hockey rinks in Canada : 3:1

Average percentage of teenagers in the world's forty-four largest countries in 1997 who recognized the Chicago Bulls's logo : 93

Average change since 1940 in worldwide IQ test scores, in points : +19

Africa

Estimated number of years by which the earliest known African ironwork predates Europe's Iron Age : 1,800

Number of civil and border wars that were being waged in Africa at the end of the twentieth century : 13

Hours after being elected president of Liberia in July 1997 that Charles G. Taylor promised not to be "a wicked president" : 1

Combined percentage of the vote won by the two opposition candidates in Tunisia's first multiparty presidential elections in 1999 : 0.56

Years after the Rwandan massacre that President Clinton admitted "we did not act quickly enough" : 4

Number of troops that could have prevented Rwanda's 1994 genocide, according to the head of U.N. forces there at the time : 5,000

Average number of prisoners per square yard in Rwanda's Gitarama prison camp in the year following the genocide : 2

Number of $3,000 hand-carved African "fantasy coffins" ordered from Neiman Marcus's 1995 Christmas catalog : 6

Rank of Africa among continents with the largest number of newly diagnosed HIV carriers : 1

Percentage of its AIDS drugs that a 1997 agreement requires South Africa to buy from U.S. companies : 100

Ratio of the price of a month's worth of U.S. AIDS drugs in South Africa to what Indian-made drugs would cost if sold there : 7:1

Amount by which U.S. exports to sub-Saharan Africa in 1998 exceeded U.S. exports to all the countries of the former Soviet Union that year : $2,100,000,000

Rank of Cameroon among countries where a government official was most likely to solicit a bribe from a business executive in 1998 : 1

Rank of Nigeria among countries that have the highest rate of regular attendance at religious services : 1

Ratio of Rwanda's 1997 GDP to Harvard University's annual budget : 1:1

Estimated number of Rwandan households headed by children in 1998 : 85,000

Chance that an African woman died from pregnancy-related causes in 1990 : 1 in 106

Minimum number of people in Sierra Leone who suffered mutilation of their arms, legs, lips, or ears by rebel forces in 1998 : 4,000

Estimated number of people in southern and central Sudan who were killed by their own government between 1983 and 1998 : 1,900,000

Number of people who died in police custody in South Africa in 1998 : 758

Maximum number of people reported to have died in custody during any year under apartheid : 200

Number of years it took South Africa's Natal Law Society to apologize for trying to prevent Mohandas K. Gandhi from practicing law there in 1894 : 105

Number of ex-inmates of South Africa's Robben Island Prison who now serve as tour guides there : 4

Number of ex-guards who do : 1

Asia

Year in which China introduced the first paper currency : 1022

Number of China's four largest banks in 1997 that were insolvent that year : 3

Ratio of the number of Chinese who owned a television set in 1995 to those who had running hot water : 84:1

Percentage of Chinese who said in 1995 that they agreed with Mao's dictum "Never think of yourself, give everything in service to society" : 4

Estimated number of Chinese who die each day from smoking-related illnesses : 2,000

Percentage of North Korea's population that died of starvation from 1994 to 1998 : 11

Average number of full-time surgeons on call in East Timor in 1999 : 1

Number of pharmacies in the Cambodian city of Angkor Thom in the thirteenth century : 102

Number of years after Jews settled in China that they were first allowed to live in Russian territory : 1,045

Change in the price of one square foot of Hong Kong office space between 1997 and the country's absorption by China in 1998 : –$1,040

Rank of Hong Kong among the countries most often visited in a professional capacity by House members in 1997 : 1

Minutes of "delightful conversation" with Pakistani Prime Minister Benazir Bhutto reported by Senator Jesse Helms in the spring of 1995 : 60

Number of minutes later that he introduced her to the Senate as the leader of India : 10

Number of members in the Hillary Rodham Clinton fan club in Bombay : 153

Percentage by which India increased the budget of its Department of Atomic Energy in 1998 : 68

Number of years that the U.S. spent training Pakistani nuclear-research scientists as part of the "Atoms for Peace" program : 19

Number of Chinese engineers who accompanied the Mongol Khan Hulägu on his siege of Baghdad in 1257 : 1,000

Number of ships that sailed in the first expedition of Cheng Ho, the fifteenth-century Chinese explorer : 287

Minimum number of countries Cheng Ho visited over the course of his seven voyages : 30

Years after Portuguese adventurers brought guns to Japan in 1543 that Japan owned more guns than any other country : 57

Estimated number of Japanese peasant uprisings in the following 268 years under the Tokugawa regime : 3,000

Number of registered swords in Japan in 1999 : 6,293

Chance that a murder there involves a gun : 1 in 73

Percentage of all criminal defendants tried in Japanese courts each year who are found guilty : 99.9

Chances that a Catholic saint canonized since 1978 is Vietnamese : 2 in 5

Percentage change in foreign direct investment in Vietnam between 1991 and 1996 : +1,142

Percentage change since then : −43

Percentage change between 1985 and 1997 in the military budget of Vietnam : −71

Percentage change in the military budget of Singapore : +144

Maximum fine for selling chewing gum there : $1,176

Fine levied against a political-opposition leader in Singapore in 1999 for publicly reading the nation's constitution aloud : $1,452

Days before Time Warner's Fortune Global Forum opened in China in 1999 that China banned *Time* magazine's special issue devoted to China : 6

Number of years in the twentieth century during which Taiwan was directly controlled by mainland China : 4

Russia

Chances that a Russian favored independence for Chechnya in 1995 : 3 in 4

Percentage of Chechnya's air force that was destroyed in September 1999 when Russia bombed a single plane : 100

Percentage of Russians who said in 1995 that their country needed "order" more than it did "democracy" : 77

Number of years after the Soviet national anthem was retired that Russia's Duma voted in 1999 to reinstate the melody : 7

Percentage increase proposed in 1994 by Russian president Boris Yeltsin in the number of signatures required to run for the Russian presidency : 1,900

Percentage increase signed into law the following year : 900

Months of prison labor to which a Russian journalist could be sentenced for ridiculing Yeltsin in 1996 : 12

Place for which Boris Yeltsin and Vladimir Zhirinovsky were tied that year, among the ten political leaders Russians most trusted : 8

Number of years by which Yeltsin has outlived the average life expectancy of a Russian male : 8

Average number of Russian soldiers who died by suicide or hazing each week in 1997 : 51

Number of the Russians injured on Moscow Metro escalators in 1984 who were drunk at the time : 84

Ratio of the amount of money Americans spent last year on alcoholic beverages to the value of the Russian stock market : 7:1

Ratio of annual U.S. trade with the countries of the former Soviet Union in 1997 to U.S. trade with Africa : 1:2.3

Ratio of Russia's estimated revenue in 1999 to New York City's revenue that year : 7:8

Percentage change between 1998 and 1999 in the number of Russians enrolled in Hebrew classes : +80

Ratio of the cost to Pizza Hut in 1999 for an ad on a Russian space rocket to the price of a 30-second Super Bowl ad that year : 1:2

Percentage change in the size of Russia's economy since the country began following the IMF's advice in 1992 : −30

Estimated portion of the value of the currency circulating in Russia in 1998 that was in U.S. dollars : ½

The Middle East

Estimated number of Planet Hollywood franchises to be opened in the Middle East in the next five years : 7

Ratio of the combined GDP of all Arab countries in the Persian Gulf to that of Belgium : 1:1

Change since 1981 in Saudi Arabia's ranking among countries with the largest cash reserves : −37

Portion of the Islamic world that was controlled by Shiites in the year 1000 : ½

Chance that a Muslim was a Shiite then : 1 in 20

Chance that a Muslim is a Shiite today : 1 in 7

Percentage change in the number of Israelis living on the West Bank since the signing of 1993's Oslo peace accords : +50

Factor by which the rate of West Bank settlement increased in the three months after Ehud Barak was elected Prime Minister of Israel in 1999 : 2.5

Percentage of Jerusalem's Jewish population that is ultra-Orthodox : 30

Percentage of Jerusalem's Jewish kindergartners who are : 52

Chance that a Jewish Jerusalemite believed in 1998 that sovereignty over the city's holy sites "ultimately belongs to God" : 1 in 3

Chances that a Palestinian Jerusalemite believed this : 2 in 3

Chances that an officer in Iran's rebel National Liberation Army is a woman : 7 in 10

Number of days an Afghani man may be imprisoned for trimming his beard : 10

Number of liposuction machines that Iraq sought U.N. permission to import in 1998 : 4

Estimated value of oil exports Iraq says it has lost per day since 1990 as a result of U.N. sanctions : $53,550,000

Percentage change in Iraqi oil sales between 1997 and 1998 : +45

Percentage change in total oil sales of other OPEC countries : −35

Percentage by which 1998 Iraqi oil sales fell short of the maximum allowed under U.N. sanctions : 22

Rank of the U.S. among countries that have bought the most oil from Iraq since 1997 : 1

Value of the U.S. military equipment earmarked in 1998 for Iraqi anti–Saddam Hussein groups : $97,000,000

Amount used through March of 1999 : $0

Minimum number of the ten biological materials suspected in Iraqi warfare research in the 1990s that were supplied by U.S. firms : 9

Number of biological materials with military potential sent to Iraq by the U.S. Centers for Disease Control and Prevention in the 1980s : 14

Ratio of Iraqi chemical-warfare agents destroyed in the Gulf War to those since destroyed under U.N. pressure : 2:5

Estimated tons of depleted uranium from rounds fired in the Gulf War that are still scattered across the battlefields : 320

Estimated number of Iraqi and Kuwaiti civilians killed by unexploded allied cluster bombs in the two years following the end of the Gulf War : 1,600

Ratio of civilians killed in April 1996 by the Israeli army in Lebanon to those killed by terrorists in Israel since 1996 : 3:2

Ratio of Palestinians to Israelis killed in political violence since the signing of the self-rule accord in 1993 : 7:5

Percentage of Palestinians who said in 1997 that they approved of suicide bombings : 24

Ratio of blank or "spoiled" ballots cast in the 1996 Israeli election to the number of votes by which Benjamin Netanyahu won : 5:1

Total number of dogs and whores of whom Yassir Arafat is the son, according to Syria's defense minister General Mustafa Tlass in 1999 : 120,000

Europe

Number of major European peasant revolutions begun between 1809 and 1848 : 8

Number of these that were begun in the name of the Catholic Church or to reinstate a deposed monarch : 7

Year in which the CIA predicted a "violent conflagration" in Yugoslavia : 1990

Year in which former Secretary of State Warren Christopher said that the "Serbian influence" in Kosovo must be limited : 1993

Estimated number of the 222,200 "armor-piercing bomblets" dropped on Kosovo in 1999 that remained unexploded six months later : 11,110

Estimated tons of high-performance explosives in the possession of the Irish Republican Army in 1999 : 2.7

Number of people who have died in three decades of fighting in Northern Ireland : 3,300

Percentage of the residents of Northern Ireland who report being happy : 92

Percentage of the residents of the rest of Ireland who do : 90

Rank of Ireland among European Union countries with the largest percentage increase in GDP in 1995 : 1

Number of Western European countries whose 1983 deficit represented a larger portion of GDP than the U.S. deficit did that year : 8

Number of Western European countries whose 1997 deficit represented a larger portion of GDP than the U.S. deficit did : 12

Percentage of Germans who believe that those who don't cheat on their taxes "deserve only pity" : 46

Percentage of French gas stations that ran dry after a five-day 1997 roadblock by striking French truckers : 40

Minimum salary for which French truckers agreed to abandon the strike : $21,000

Number of days in 1998 during which Norway's Prime Minister Kjell Bondevik was too depressed to work : 24

Number of years former Serbian leader and indicted war criminal Radovan Karadzic spent practicing psychiatry : 20

Estimated number of professional "occultists" practicing in France : 50,000

Estimated ratio of active, full-time cricket players in the U.S. to the number of Druids in Britain : 1:1

Estimated ratio of German autoworkers to German environmental workers : 7:10

Number of French job seekers whose résumés were printed on wine bottles by local vintners in the spring of 1995 : 1,000

Number of German police officers who lived with immigrants in Bonn for a week in 1996 for "sensitivity training" : 10

Number of years since then that the training has been repeated : 0

Number of Fiat owners Paris police were ordered to question in connection with Princess Diana's death : 40,000

Days in jail to which a British retiree was sentenced in 1996 for excessive pigeon feeding : 56

Months two British neighbors spent hooting at owls at night before realizing that they were hooting at each other : 12

Estimated amount the BBC paid for noise-producing software in 1999 after workers complained of the quiet : $1,600

Number of radio and television stations shut down by the Yugoslav government during the 1999 NATO bombardment : 10

Maximum size in square meters of a new suburban shopping mall in Norway, according to legislation passed last year : 3,000

Maximum fine to which a British grocer will be subject next year for using anything other than the metric system : £5,000

Minimum length the European Committee for Standardization set for condoms, in inches : 6.8

Maximum months of maternity leave Croatia's "family values" plan allows an employed, pregnant mother of two : 36

Percentage of British Parliament members who believed in 1996 that stress was reducing their interest in sex : 38

Number of political parties represented by the 5,065 candidates running for the German legislature in 1997 : 34

Estimated change since 1984 in the number of Alcoholics Anonymous groups in Poland : +1,473

Minimum number of brands of bottled water available on a given day at Amsterdam's Waterwinkel boutique : 90

Ratio of the amount Britons spent on lottery tickets last year to the amount they spent on tea : 5:1

Number of people waiting to get on the official waiting list of Britain's National Health Service during the last year of the Tory government : 247,500

Number of people waiting to get on the waiting list under Labour in 1998 : 334,000

Ratio of the average volume of a breast implant inserted in the U.S. to that of one inserted in Europe : 3:2

Number of European countries with worse adult literacy rates than England : 2

Percentage of Britons between the ages of eleven and fourteen in 1995 who could not identify Winston Churchill : 31

Age at which Northern Ireland's new minister of education, former I.R.A. commander Martin McGuinness, dropped out of school : 15

Estimated number of years that Ireland's Sinn Fein leader Gerry Adams received British public assistance : 10

Number of years British Prime Minister Tony Blair served as lead singer of the rock band Ugly Rumours : 2

Number of ornamental figures based on German Chancellor Helmut Kohl in Germany's Garden Gnome Museum in 1998 : 14

Percentage change in sales of cream cakes baked in the Pope's hometown in the three months after his endorsement of them in June 1999 : +1,150

Amount British Nuclear Fuels paid the British Scouts in 1997 to add its logo to their scientist badge : $49,776

Number of years Jeanne Louise Calment, France's oldest woman, smoked cigarettes before she quit in 1993 : 97

Number of years later that she died : 4

Average number of people who break bones or are hospitalized each year after slipping on dog feces in Paris : 650

Latin America and the Caribbean

Average percentage change, during NAFTA's first year, in top executive salaries at the twenty-six largest firms in Mexico : +29

Average percentage of the raw materials processed by Mexican maquiladoras since NAFTA went into effect that came from Mexican suppliers : 2

Average percentage before NAFTA : 1.5

Percentage change in the total value of raw materials processed by Mexican maquiladoras since 1980 : +2,072

Percentage change in the number of joint ventures between Cuba and foreign companies between 1992 and 1999 : +886

Amount for which Cuba has announced it will sue the U.S. over casualties caused by the thirty-nine-year trade embargo : $181,100,000,000

Estimated chance that a Cuban worker is paid in currency other than the Cuban peso : 1 in 4

Average hourly outflow from Brazil's currency reserves in the two days following the devaluation of the country's currency : $214,000,000

Estimated percentage change between 1991 and 1995 in the number of Brazilian workers engaged in forced labor : +533

Minimum number of laws passed in Peru since 1992 that violate at least one article of the country's constitution : 91

Number of independent candidates not included on the ballot during Haiti's national elections in 1995 : 112

Chance that an eligible Haitian voter participated in the country's national elections two years later : 1 in 20

Points by which the percentage of Mexican adults who are registered to vote exceeds the percentage of Americans who are : 30

Number of the eight Zapatista demands to which the Mexican government agreed in 1996 that have been met : 0

Number of face masks that Mexico's Zapatista leader Subcommandante Marcos has worn out since 1994 : 5

Number of weapons depicted on Haiti's national flag : 10

Last year in which President Clinton gave a speech in which he referred to U.S. intervention in Haiti as a "success" : 1996

Estimated percentage of adult Haitians who were unemployed in 1998 : 65

Ratio of total U.S. disaster aid to Honduras in 1998 to average annual U.S. military aid to Honduras in the 1980s : 6:7

Ratio of the number of calories a Cuban consumes each day to the number an American does : 1:2

Ratio of the number of doctors per capita in Cuba to the number in the U.S. : 2:1

Ratio of Cuba's infant mortality rate to that of the U.S. : 1:1

Ratio of professional jobs available in Mexico in the 1980s to the number of Mexicans who graduated from college then: 1:4

Weeks after Fausto Alzatti was appointed Mexico's secretary of education in 1994 that he admitted he had no college degree : 6

Days after Mexico's drug czar was arrested for corruption in 1997 that his lawyer was arrested for bribing jurors : 165

Percentage change in Colombia's estimated cocaine production since 1990 : +154

Average number of kidnappings reported in Colombia each day in 1999 : 8

Percentage of crimes reported in Mexico City since 1992 that have been solved : 3.7

Number of Mexico's federal law-enforcement agents reprimanded in 1996 for violating "ethical standards" : 1,118

Estimated cost of sealing the U.S.-Mexican border with a replica of the Great Wall of China : $45,000,000,000

Migration

Years by which new evidence suggests that the age of the first human migration to the Americas should be increased : 20,000

Portion of U.S. citizens whose ancestors came through Ellis Island : ⅖

Chance that a U.S. urban public-school student in 1909 was born to immigrants: 1 in 2

Chance in 1995 : 1 in 18

Rank of Asia among the continents of origin of the most highly educated immigrants to the U.S. in 1997 : 1

Chance a U.S. Econo-Lodge franchise is owned by an Indian American : 1 in 2

Chance that a Kosovar refugee crossing the Serbian border in April 1999 was a child : 1 in 2

Chance that an ethnic Albanian left Kosovo while Serbian troops controlled the region in the spring of 1999 : 1 in 2

Chance that a Serb left the region within four months after NATO troops took it over in June of that year : 1 in 2

Percentage change since 1992 in the number of asylum applications made to European countries : −52

Ratio of the number of Jews living in Germany in 1990 to the number living there in 1995 : 1:2

Estimated number of U.S. Christians who moved to Jerusalem's Mount of Olives in 1998 and 1999 to await the millennium : 200

Amount by which the number of emigrants from the U.S. to Ireland between 1995 and 1998 exceeded those from Ireland to the U.S. : 4,300

Percentage change since 1996 in the amount of time it takes a U.S. green-card holder to become a resident : +100

Percentage change since 1992 in the green-card application fee charged by the Immigration and Naturalization Service : +70

Percentage change since 1994 in the number of beds in INS detention facilities : +282

Chance that a U.S. federal prison inmate is not a U.S. citizen : 1 in 4

Estimated number of undocumented migrants who died between 1993 and 1998 while trying to cross the U.S.-Mexican border : 1,185

Number of Texas and California counties colonized by African "killer" bees since 1994 : 51

Average number of non-native insect species entering Hawaii each year : 17.5

Estimated number of non-native species that have entered the North American ecosystem since 1500 : 50,000

Average number of Americans who emigrate each day : 770

Transportation

Chance that an American fell asleep at the wheel last year : 1 in 4

Blood-alcohol level a driver would need in order to be as dangerous as a driver using a cellular phone : 0.1

Average number of potholes per mile of paved U.S. road : 13

Amount the U.S. spends on road construction and maintenance each day : $206,000,000

Ratio of highway spending Congress approved in 1998 to the cost of gold-plating one lane of the U.S. interstate system : 2:1

Maximum legal length, in feet, of a limousine in California: 65

Length, in feet, of the longest one available for rental there : 66.5

Factor by which the average air-pollution levels inside a moving car on an L.A. highway exceed those of the air outside the car : 10

Estimated number of cans of Campbell's cream of mushroom soup spilled on a San Diego interstate in February 1997 : 55,800

Hours that three miles of Nebraska's Route 83 were closed in the fall of 1996 when a truck carrying two nuclear bombs overturned : 2

Number of chapels built at U.S. truckstops since 1981 by Truckstop Ministries : 51

Number of states where legislation forbidding discrimination against motorcyclists has been introduced since 1998 : 10

Percentage of people using the bathroom in New York's Penn Station who do not wash their hands : 40

Number of air-traffic controllers ordered to take a two-hour "refresher" course in 1998 : 10,000

Number of times that year that air-traffic controllers lost track of the altitude or speed of Air Force I or II : 4

Number of U.S. Congress members who died in plane crashes in the twentieth century : 17

Ratio of the number of Americans killed in traffic accidents in 1998 to the number killed by medical errors that year : 1:1

Rank of Aries among the astrological signs of people most likely to be in an automobile accident : 1

Percentage change since 1990 in the number of U.S. traffic disputes in which one driver kills or injures another : +59

Percentage change between 1983 and 1995 in the average number of times a U.S. household uses its car each day : +56

Chance that a Detroit household has no access to a car : 1 in 3

Rank of Detroit, among the twenty largest U.S. cities, in annual municipal spending on public transportation : 20

Percentage increase since 1994 in annual federal spending on mass transit and highways, respectively : 33,50

Percentage of all commuter trips taken in 1980 that were in carpools : 20

Percentage today : 13

Maximum business deduction allowed U.S. employers in 1998 for each employee parking space they provided : $175

Maximum deduction allowed employers that year for van-pool or mass-transit expenses, per employee : $65

Number of the ten largest multinational corporations that produce automobiles or gasoline : 9

Gallons of red wine the city of Stockholm purchased in 1995 for conversion into ethanol to fuel its public buses : 750,000

Year in which England repealed a law mandating an "orderly, proper line" at bus stops : 1995

Hours during which Rio de Janeiro drivers may legally run red lights in order to avoid being carjacked : 10 P.M.–5 A.M.

Percentage change in retail car sales in Mexico in the year after the 1994 peso collapse : −42

Average annual interest rate on a car loan in Mexico in 1995 : 102

Average age, in years, of a car registered in the U.S. in 1998 : 9

Last year in which the average U.S. car was this old : 1948

Hours it took six residents of May Valley, Washington, to renovate a local intersection in 1995 after waiting ten years for the state to do it : 6

Number of federally maintained bridges of which the Department of Transportation had no record in 1998 : 4,770

Ratio of the projected construction cost of the L.A. subway system to the cost of one space-shuttle launch : 10:1

American Pie

Hours an Oklahoma teenager was detained by police in 1996 after wiping his dipstick with an American flag : 2.5

Number of states that require fingerprinting of all driver's-license applicants : 5

Miles of asphalt road in the U.S. the year Senator Strom Thurmond was born : 18

Miles that Leif Eriksson sailed from his father's home in Greenland before "discovering" North America in 985 : 230

Portion of California's revenue between 1852 and 1870 that came from taxes paid by Chinese laborers : ½

Number of times that California's governor has declared a state of emergency since 1990 : 34

Ratio of federal emergency spending appropriated for 1999 to the average annual appropriation in the previous five years : 5:2

Rank of the U.S., among G-7 nations, in investment in public infrastructure : 7

Portion of U.S. currency held overseas in 1970 : $\frac{1}{10}$

Portion today : $\frac{1}{2}$

Chances that an adult white male in eighteenth-century Pennsylvania was not allowed to own a gun as a result of refusing to take a loyalty oath : 2 in 5

Estimated number of years that Virginia used tobacco as a currency : 200

Acres of hemp grown by "patriotic" U.S. farmers in 1942 at the behest of the U.S. government : 36,000

Number of non-military federal agencies whose officers have the authority to carry firearms and make arrests : 63

Number of military agencies whose officers may do so : 16

Percentage change since 1970 in the number of nongovernmental organizations operating in the U.S. : +57

Minimum estimated number of them that sent representatives to 1999's WTO conference in Seattle : 800

Percentage change between 1994 and 1998 in the annual number of independent commercial banks opening in the U.S. : +276

Number of U.S. banks in 1921 and 1933, respectively : 30,456, 14,207

Number today : 8,675

Ratio of federal spending in 1999 on foreign aid to federal spending on the Corporation for Public Broadcasting : 54:1

Percentage of Americans who believe that the media "hurt democracy" : 38

Duration in days of the 1996 standoff between federal agents and members of the Montana Freemen holed up at Ralph Clark's ranch in Jordan, Montana : 81

Farm subsidies received by Clark during the previous ten years : $676,082

Median annual income Americans believed they would need to fulfill their "dreams" in 1994 : $102,200

Percentage change between 1993 and 1994 in the number of Americans who said they would require $1 million to do so : +75

Tons of clothing and footwear disposed of in U.S. landfills or incinerators in 1998 : 5,200,000

Salary cap for all Americans proposed by Louisiana senator Huey Long in 1932 : $1,000,000

Number of years later that he was murdered : 3.3

Average number of Americans killed each year by private citizens using guns in self-defense : 262

Average number who use guns each year to commit suicide : 18,000

Chance that a U.S. shooting death is a suicide : 1 in 2

Estimated chance that a U.S. Muslim is of Arab descent : 1 in 5

Number of "non-white" ethnic or racial groups that Denny's owners comprise : 85

Average percentage by which white Americans overestimate the Latino, Asian-, and African-American populations : 100

Average percentage by which members of these groups over-estimate their own populations : 100

Chance that a Mexican lives in a non-metropolitan area : 1 in 4

Chance that an American does : 1 in 5

Percentage of U.S. adults in 1995 who could not identify the president of Mexico : 98

Number of U.S. presidents besides Bill Clinton who have made an official visit to an Indian reservation since 1937 : 0

Price a Pennsylvania company charged in 1999 for one buffalo, "butchered, portioned, and shipped . . . the ultimate gift of the new millennium" : $15,000

Amount for which a North Dakota town agreed in 1998 to rename itself after a brand of schnapps for four years : $100,000

Weight, in pounds, of an apple pie baked by students at Spokane Community College in July 1994 : 33,500

New York, New York

Number of times since 1994 that the ACLU has taken New York City Mayor Rudolph Giuliani to court : 20

Number of times it has won : 17

Percentage change in murder, rape, and robbery cases in New York City during Giuliani's first two years as mayor : −28

Percentage change during that time in the number of allega-tions of excessive force made against the city's police : +62

Percentage change since 1989 in the amount the city pays out each year in police abuse settlements : +344

Percentage change since 1993 in the annual number of criminal cases dismissed by New York City judges : +132

Average number of arrests made by the NYPD in 1998 for every crime reported : 1.1

Estimated number of strip searches conducted on people held in non-felony arrests in city jails in 1996 and 1997 : 87,000

Number of surveillance cameras monitoring the city's public spaces : 2,397

Percentage that are privately owned : 88

Number of Manhattan pedestrians splattered with blood in 1998 by a suicide's seventeen-story jump : 3

Number of objects made with human dung in the permanent collection of the Brooklyn Museum of Art : 4

Average number of death threats received each week in 1999 by Mayor Giuliani : 2

Miles per hour at which a New York TV station clocked a police van driving Giuliani to lunch in 1998 : 75

Number of earthquakes measuring between three and five on the Richter scale that have hit the New York City area in the last twenty years : 16

Amount Con Edison paid to design and produce 150 "special millennial edition manhole covers" to be installed in New York City in 2000 : $28,600

Chance that a child born in New York City in 1998 is living in poverty : 1 in 2

Chance that a Yankee Stadium ticket for the 1998 World Series games was available to the public : 1 in 6

Rank of Manhattan among U.S. counties with the largest income gap between rich and poor : 2

Estimated revenue that the U.N. generates each year for New York City : $3,300,000,000

Percentage change since 1965 in the number of the city's kosher delis : −76

Number of Astoria Federal Savings ATMs at which transactions may be conducted in Yiddish : 25

Lines of Walt Whitman poetry entered as evidence in New York's dispute with New Jersey over Ellis Island : 37

Rank of New York City, among urban habitats worldwide with the largest number of peregrine falcons per square mile : 1

Ratio of the number of New Yorkers bitten by rats in 1997 to the number bitten by other New Yorkers : 1:7

Pounds of yak hair used in the Broadway production of *Cats* since 1982 : 3,067

Gallons of chewing gum scraped up each year by the maintenance crew at the Statue of Liberty : 39

Going South

Number of Tennessee state senators who voted against a 1996 bill urging businesses to post the Ten Commandments : 1

Blocks from Abraham Lincoln's tomb that a notice was posted in 1995 warning cabdrivers not to pick up black males : 14

Estimated number of days later that the capital's Lincoln Yellow Cab Company agreed to "monitor" its bulletin board : 48

Chance that an African-American man in Alabama is ineligible to vote because of former or current imprisonment : 1 in 3

Percentage of Alabamans who oppose removing the state's constitutional ban on "interracial" marriage : 26

Number of Washington, D.C., police assigned to a 1999 neo-Nazi American Nationalist Party march : 1,426

Number of marchers who showed up : 4

Number of the 15,896 students in Washington, D.C., public high schools in 1999 who were white : 460

Number of textbook reproductions of *George Washington Crossing the Delaware* that were retouched by a Georgia school in 1999 : 2,322

Number of parental complaints that prompted the school to determine that Washington's watch fob resembled genitalia : 0

Number of men ticketed for indecent exposure in Opelousas, Louisiana, in 1998 for wearing low-riding pants : 14

Maximum fine for begging without a permit in Orlando, Florida : $500

Federal anti-poverty funds granted Texas since 1996 that had not been spent by the fall of 1999 : $149,000,000

Average number of baptisms performed at Southern Baptist churches each day in 1998 : 1,129

Chance that a New Orleans tree is infested with Formosan termites : 1 in 5

Rank of Atlanta among U.S. cities in the number of miles driven per capita : 1

Number of people in North Carolina killed by automobiles since 1998 after lying in the middle of the road : 66

Number of "I Slept With Kenneth Starr" bumper stickers sold by a Little Rock gift shop between March and August of 1998 : 990

Price of a dozen rolls of "Helms Happens" toilet paper, plus shipping and handling : $25

Number of days in 1998 that Senator Trent Lott successfully lobbied Congress to extend three Southern states' duck-hunting seasons : 14

Amount an Alabama church raised in 1994 by staging a "Coon Hunt for Christ" : $2,500

Number of convicted felons elected as Mississippi county sheriffs in 1996 : 3

COMMUNICATIONS

News

The Tube

Hollywood

Music

Reading and Writing

In the Mail

On the Wire

Talk

News

Chance that an American believes freedom of the press should be "protected in all circumstances" : 1 in 3

Chance that an American cannot name a single right protected by the First Amendment : 1 in 3

Amount by which sales of the 1995 issue of the *Washington Post* that contained the Unabomber's tract exceeded average daily sales : 16,000

Average percentage of local-TV evening news time in January 1995 that was devoted to crime and disaster coverage : 53

Average percentage of local-TV evening news time in March 1998 that was devoted to crime and disaster coverage : 40

Chance that a U.S. newspaper publisher believed in 1998 that coverage of important news is often "shallow and inadequate" : 1 in 2

Median jury award made against a U.S. news media company in 1990 : $550,000

Median award in 1997 : $2,600,000

Percentage of local-TV news directors who say their stations have been sued for libel since 1995 : 38

Percentage who say they have dropped "important information" from a story since then for fear of being sued : 28

Years after a 1938 Johns Hopkins study found that smoking shortens human life that any major U.S. media outlet reported it : 14

Number of news stories published between 1991 and Princess Diana's death containing the words "princess" and "colonic irrigation" : 243

Percentage of Americans in 1995 who believed that journalists are more cynical than other professionals : 45

Percentage of journalists who believed this : 54

Ratio of Americans who say they trust TV news magazines to those who say they trust print news magazines : 2:1

Ratio of those who say they trust local TV news to those who say they trust C-SPAN : 2:1

Year in which United Press International recommended to its writers that their articles not exceed 300 words : 1997

Percentage change since 1990 in minutes of network news devoted to stories broadcast from foreign bureaus: −62

Percentage change between 1992 and 1994 in the circulation of *Pravda* : −85

Number of Moscow's major newspapers that mentioned the 1998 Clinton/Yeltsin summit on Russia's economic crisis the day before it began : 0

Number of stories about Hillary Clinton's attendance of the U.N.'s 1995 women's conference in China that appeared on Chinese TV : 0

Number of articles published between 1990 and 1996 that mention the danger of standing between Senator Phil Gramm and a camera : 19

Amount that CBS News has paid Rome's Atlante Star Hotel to use its rooftop view of St. Peter's when the Pope dies : $180,000

Number of viewers who called CBS during Connie Chung's 1995 coverage of the Oklahoma bombing to ask if Dan Rather was dead : 3

Chance that an American with a 1994 B.A. in journalism was unemployed or working in public relations or advertising by 1996 : 1 in 3

The Tube

Ratio of *America's Most Wanted* episodes aired since 1988 to the number of profiled criminals arrested since then : 1:1

Number of U.S. households that chose to watch professional wrestling over the President's 1998 televised apology regarding Monica Lewinsky : 6,379,000

Ratio of the 1998 federal budget to the total amount Americans would earn if paid the minimum wage for watching TV : 6:5

Percentage of U.S. households that contained at least three TV sets in 1990 : 24

Percentage that did in 1998 : 40

Percentage of U.S. adults who said in 1995 that they could not "survive" without a television set : 19

Minimum number of TV markets in which a 1999 FCC vote allows networks to own more than one station : 50

Days after the FCC vote that a TV executive told the *New York Times* that he was eager to play the "duopoly game" : 1

Change in the number of Americans able to receive C-SPAN full-time since Congress altered cable laws in 1992 :
−5,000,000

Annual percentage of regular public-TV viewers who donate money to their local station : 8

Percentage change between 1998 and 1999 in the number of network sitcoms whose main characters are members of the same family : −25

Percentage of Americans who had watched *Seinfeld* who said they would miss it "not very much" or "not at all" when it ceased production in 1998 : 51

Percentage who answered "no" when asked if they would like to have friends like the characters on the show : 54

Rank of *ER* among prime-time TV shows most popular with African-American viewers in 1998 : 19

Percentage of U.S. *ER* viewers who say they learn important health-care information from the show : 53

Number of reports of U.S. children crushed to death by television sets filed with the federal government between 1990 and 1997 : 28

Estimated percentage of all U.S. television cartoon programs that are drawn in Asia : 99

Number of channels offered when TV came to Fiji's Nadroga province in 1995 : 1

Percentage increase since then in the incidence of self-induced vomiting among girls there : +300

Number of countries worldwide that carry *Baywatch* : 106

Amount the U.S. government spends each year to broadcast anti-Castro TV Martí to Cuba : $11,100,000

Number of minutes that Mir's Russian cosmonauts spent advertising a "space pen" live on QVC while orbiting the earth in 1998 : 15

Number of *Jeopardy!* championships won by freshman Democratic Representative Rush Holdt : 5

Number of actors who auditioned in 1997 to be the new Captain Kangaroo : 1,000

Hollywood

Ratio of the amount of screen time devoted to dinosaurs eating people in *Lost World* to the amount of time devoted to this in *Jurassic Park* : 7:1

Decibels by which the monster's scream in the 1998 remake of *Godzilla* exceeds that of a jackhammer : 18

Minutes by which the running time of 1997's *Titanic* exceeds the time it took the ship to sink in 1912 : 40

Percentage by which the cost of producing *Titanic* exceeded the 1997 budget of the National Endowment for the Arts : 100

Ratio of the cost of making the film *Volcano* to the property damage caused by the 1980 eruption of Mount St. Helen's : 1:1

Ratio of the production cost of *The Blair Witch Project* to that of *The Haunting* : 1:2,166

Ratio of *The Blair Witch Project*'s domestic box-office receipts to those of *The Haunting* : 14:9

Percentage by which box-office receipts at theaters running the trailer for *Star Wars Episode 1* rose on the day of its 1998 release: 25

Portion of the audience at New York's Ziegfeld Theatre that day who left before the feature film began : ⅓

Year in which California Representative Bob Dornan starred in the Hollywood war film *The Starfighters* : 1964

Percentage of children between six and nine who know that Jerry Lewis was the star of the original *Nutty Professor* : 66

Average age at which an actress won an Academy Award for a leading role during the 1980s : 40

Average age at which an actress won the award in the 1990s : 37

Chance that a movie script copyrighted in the U.S. before 1925 was written by a woman : 1 in 2

Chance that watching *The Bridges of Madison County* will bring a man to tears : 1 in 2

Price of an "authentic" piece of a renovated Madison County bridge in 1995 : $16.95

Price paid at auction in 1996 for the two fiberglass tablets used in the 1956 film *The Ten Commandments* : $81,700

Chances that a U.S. film featuring male Arab or Muslim characters depicts them as greedy, violent, or dishonest : 19 in 20

Estimated number of killings in *True Lies*, a film Bob Dole cited in 1995 as among those "most friendly to the family" : 94

Minutes of airtime C-SPAN devoted in June, 1995, to a National Press Club discussion of Bob Dole by film critics Siskel and Ebert : 64

Percentage change between 1994 and 1998 in the number of G-rated feature films released by U.S. studios : +160

Percentage change since 1983 in the number of jobs in the U.S. film-production industry : +175

Years of labor at 1996's minimum wage required to earn what Disney gave Mike Ovitz as a separation package that year : 6,708

Amount that a Disney licensing agreement has earned the Royal Canadian Mounted Police since 1995 : $348,536

Number of pounds John Candy's *Canadian Bacon* body double lost in the two years following Candy's death : 243

Music

Ratio of the number of Frank Sinatra's gold records to those of Kiss : 1:1

Number of tickets to U2's forty-six North American concerts in 1997 that went unsold : 231,818

Rank of Ringo among ex-Beatles who have toured most often in the last decade : 1

Number of ads for Ringo Starr's Private Issue credit card aired during the 1995 broadcast of a six-hour Beatles documentary : 6

Price charged by a North Carolina company in 1996 for a ten-inch Chia Garcia, a bust of Jerry Garcia seeded to sprout green hair : $21.95

Hours after the 1999 Woodstock riots that a participant told a reporter that he couldn't wait to watch them on TV : 6

Number of times an Akron radio station played "Take Me Out to the Ballgame" during 1994's baseball strike : 57,161

Number of the 14 employees at Hawaii's last ukulele factory who are hearing-impaired : 5

Age at which violinist Yehudi Menuhin was told by Albert Einstein that his playing proved there was a "God in heaven" : 12

Estimated number of CAT scans a Minneapolis radiologist has performed on violins since 1989 : 50

Number of the four best-selling classical albums of all time that are collections put out by Victoria's Secret : 2

Number of CDs of inspirational or patriotic music for which Senator Orrin Hatch composed lyrics : 6

Number of temporary tattoos sported by Pat Boone during performances promoting his 1997 album, *In a Metal Mood* : 12

Chances that a hard-core rap album sold in the U.S. in 1994 was purchased by a white person : 3 in 4

Price charged by image consultancy Double XXposure to teach etiquette to R&B, hip-hop, rap, and gospel artists, per class : $250

Percentage of major U.S. recording labels that use the parental advisory stickers advocated by Tipper Gore in 1985 : 100

Years after Frank Zappa called Gore's campaign "extortion" that his daughter Diva recorded a single featuring Gore on drums : 14

Amount Bill Clinton earned in 1997 in residuals for his 1992 saxophone performance on *The Arsenio Hall Show* : $76

Number of sets played by Roger Clinton's band at the 1995 opening of the Nixon Library's "Rockin' the White House" exhibit : 1

Rank of "You'll Never Walk Alone" among Bob Dole's favorite songs : 1

Reading and Writing

Chances that a U.S. adult can't identify the source of the phrase "life, liberty, and the pursuit of happiness" : 7 in 10

Number of the two memoirs published by GOP presidential candidates in 1999 that use the phrase "toga party" : 2

Copies of *Songs for the Open Road: Poems of Travel & Adventure* with which Volkswagen equipped its 1999 cars : 40,000

Chance that a Canadian adult under the age of twenty-five believes that Allen Ginsberg was Canadian : 1 in 5

Number of California library books of modern American poetry from which pages were stolen in the first six months of 1995 : 250

Number of Boston library workers who required counseling in 1998 after a flood soaked 50,000 cartons of books : 12

Number of Library of Congress employees required to take psychological exams between 1990 and 1995 : 27

Amount the Library of Congress spent in 1997 to create a braille edition of *Playboy* : $72,000

Number of *Playboy* centerfold models since 1959 whose bios claimed their favorite book was by Ayn Rand : 12

Number of people on the Omaha, Nebraska, Public Library's waiting list to check out Madonna's book *Sex* in 1996 : 230

Number of copies that borrowers never returned : 3

Number of pages on which the phrase "you will" appears in Bill Gates's 1995 book, *The Road Ahead* : 229

Number of years after North America's first library opened in 1638 that it published a subject guide : 152

Months after publishing *The Communist Manifesto* that Karl Marx became editor of a newspaper funded by industrialists : 2

Percentage of the senior editorial staff of *Talk* magazine that resigned in the magazine's first six months of publication : 26

Chances that a hard-cover edition of Newt Gingrich's novel *1945* was returned to the publisher unsold : 4 in 5

Average number of books signed per minute by Newt Gingrich at a Boston bookstore in August 1995 : 4

Average number of books signed per minute by Colin Powell at the same store in September : 11

First prize offered in the annual Colin L. Powell Joint Warfighting Essay Contest, established in 1994 : $2,500

Ratio of the number of entries received in the contest's first year to the average annual number received since then : 5:2

Copies of Muammar Qaddafi's first short-story collection sold in Egypt in the three months following its March 1996 publication : 200,000

Portion of the words in *Webster's New World Dictionary* memorized by one non-English-speaking Thai Scrabble champ : ⅔

Percentage of the tiles included in Scrabble games produced in the U.S. that are now made in China : 100

Copies of the premier issue of the Russian-language edition of *Cosmopolitan* that were sold in Russia in 1994 : 60,000

Percentage change in its Russian circulation by 1998 : +566

Estimated number of books banned between 1965 and 1995 in Indonesia: 2,000

Estimated number of illiterates in India's population when it reached one billion in August 1999 : 300,000,000

Number of poets-in-residence sponsored by Britain's National Lottery in 1998 : 4

Number of trademarks applied for through September 1999 for use of the word "millennium" : 1,523

Number applied for by then for use of "millenium" : 199

Number of words devoted to the Depression in Houghton Mifflin's fifth-grade history book, *Build Our Nation* : 332

Number devoted to the baseball career of Cal Ripken Jr. : 339

Average grade level at which a Washington, D.C., inmate can read : 3

Average grade level at which he or she left school : 8

Number of words in the 1999 *Merriam-Webster Collegiate Dictionary* whose "offensive" designation is italicized : 200

Years of editorial consideration preceding the inclusion of the word "phat" in Random House's 1996 *Compact Unabridged Dictionary* : 4

Estimated number of changes made to James Joyce's *Ulysses* for a "people's edition" published in 1997 : 9,000

In the Mail

Number of credit-card solicitations mailed to Americans in 1997 : 3,000,000,000

Number of U.S. zip codes accounted for by the Pentagon : 4

Number of foreign embassies that received GOP fund-raising letters in October 1997 : 30

Suggested annual donation each letter requested : $5,000

Length, in pages, of the letter Linda Tripp distributed in the winter of 1998 soliciting donations to her legal defense fund : 12

Number of Americans who had made a donation by February 1999 : 20,000

Number of people on the mailing list of the World Canine Freestyle Organization, a group devoted to dancing with dogs : 8,000

Number of subscribers to *Eternal Ink*, the official newsletter of the Christian Tattoo Association : 23

Number of 1998 mail-order catalogues from the L.A. County Coroner's gift shop distributed worldwide : 21,000

Percentage increase since 1994 in the annual number of catalogues the gift shop distributes : 110

Price paid at an auction in 1997 for a letter from Madonna to Dennis Rodman : $5,175

Price paid at auction that year for a letter from Eleanor Roosevelt to an editor of *Woman's Wear News* : $230

Letters of complaint elicited by a *Dr. Quinn, Medicine Woman* episode in which the doctor supports the theory of evolution : 80

Letters of complaint the show received about an episode in which Walt Whitman takes Dr. Quinn's son camping : 94

Number of greeting cards for "non-traditional families" introduced by Hallmark in 1999 : 104

On the Wire

Chances that a human being alive today has never made a telephone call : 2 in 3

Ratio of the number of telephone lines in sub-Saharan Africa to the number in Manhattan : 2:3

Years it took Afghanistan to restore its international phone links after civil war disabled them in 1993 : 7

Average number of minutes per day that Americans spend waiting for Web pages to download : 9

Average number of prayers sent to the Wailing Wall each day via e-mail : 100

Estimated amount U.S. telephone companies grossed in 1998 from phone calls made by prisoners : $840,000,000

Estimated profit to New York State from collect calls placed by inmates last year : $21,000,000

Minimum cost of an autopsy from 1-800-AUTOPSY : $2,000

Percentage change since 1996 in the number of U.S. adults who use the Internet to obtain health-care information : +218

Number of subscribers to PursuitWatch, an L.A. paging service that alerts customers when a high-speed chase is televised : 350

Number of subscribers in 1994 to Call of the Wind, a California paging service that alerts windsurfers to good conditions : 200

Number in 1999 : 1,750

Fee charged by an L.A. cyberpsychologist for online treatment of Internet addiction, per minute : $1.08

Estimated number of people who watched a live Webcast of a hair transplant in the fall of 1998 : 8,000

Factor by which online campaign contributions to Al Gore in 1999 exceeded online contributions to George W. Bush : 5

Average amount a member of Congress received from telecommunications-industry PACs between 1985 and 1994 : $22,464

Fine that the 1998 Internet posting of the Starr Report might have brought Congress if 1996's Communications Decency Act had become law : $250,000

Percentage of House members who voted for both the Communications Decency Act and the report's release : 66

Number of the seven dedicated phone lines linking U.S. and Russian leaders that were Y2K compliant by October 1999 : 1

Year in which the partially state-owned China Internet Corporation acquired the domain name Taiwan.com : 1994

Maximum number of years to which a Burmese citizen can be sentenced for owning an unregistered computer : 15

Estimated number of "objectionable" Web pages to which The Learning Company's Cyber Patrol software blocks access : 8,000,000

Year in which all mobile-phone companies will be federally required to be able to locate callers within 125 feet : 2002

Price in 1999 of the Truth Phone, a lie detector for the telephone, from the Counter Spy Shop in Washington, D.C. : $3,900

Chance that a U.S. man's method of breaking off a relationship is to "just stop calling" : 1 in 10

Talk

Percentage of Americans who say that they speak English "very well" : 94

Number of African languages added to the U.S. Census Bureau Language Program since 1990 : 5

Number of Eastern European languages dropped from the program by 1999 : 3

Number of the fifteen languages used in ads for the 2000 Census that are Asian: 10

Percentage change in enrollment in U.S. college-level French and German courses since 1995 : –4.5

Percentage change in enrollment in Arabic and Biblical Hebrew courses : +44.7

Number of the world's 6,000 living languages that are indigenous to Papua, New Guinea : 1,000

Year in which the word "homesick" was coined : 1798

Chance that an evil character in a Disney animated movie speaks with a foreign accent : 1 in 2

Hours of study required to lose a Long Island accent, according to Long Island's Professional Voice Care Center : 26

Year in which Tupperware began training its sales staff to use the word "whisper" rather than "burp" in describing the sound of air escaping from its containers : 1990

Number of Shakespeare's thirty-seven plays that West Virginia senator Robert Byrd has quoted on the Senate floor : 37

Rank of the 104th, among congresses elected since 1984 in which the word "scum" was used most often in session : 1

Months after publicly calling President Clinton a "scumbag" in 1998 that Congressman Dan Burton admitted to being an adulterer : 4

Ratio of times a member of Congress was accused of being a "liar" in the 104th session to the times a foreigner was : 4:1

Average ratio in the preceding five sessions : 1:5

Rank of "intelligent," "smart," and "bitch" among the words that Americans believed best described Hillary Rodham Clinton in 1996 : 1,2,3

Rank of "rich," "crazy," and "idiot" among those Americans believed best described Ross Perot : 1,2,3

Year in which George W. Bush first described juvenile "super-predators" as "fatherless, jobless, fearless, and godless" : 1996

Number of federal candidates publicly declared to have "crossed a Rubicon" while campaigning in 1999 : 3

Percentage of radio-talk-show listeners in 1995 who blamed the "mainstream media" for the Oklahoma City bombing : 15

Chance that a U.S. adult could not define the term "channel surfing" that year : 1 in 3

Chances that a U.S. child over the age of nine that year could not define the word "Internet" : 5 in 6

Age at which Al Sharpton preached his first sermon : 4

Age at which Albert Einstein spoke his first words : 3

ECONOMICS

Wealth and Poverty

Taxes

IOUs

Imports and Exports

Speculation

The Corporate World

On the Job

Shopping

Wealth and Poverty

Rank of the U.S. among the seventeen leading industrial nations with the largest percentage of their populations in poverty : 1

Rank of the U.S. among G-7 countries in 1996 whose deficit represented the smallest percentage of GDP : 1

Ratio of the size of the national debt in 1998 to the net worth of the richest 1 percent of U.S. households that year : 1:2

Average amount each American living in poverty would receive if 1998's budget surplus had been divided among them : $1,967

Percentage of the poverty level for a family of three earned by a full-time minimum-wage worker in 1998 : 82

Percentage of the 1968 poverty level earned by a full-time minimum-wage worker that year : 111

Ratio of Americans earning less than $23,800 per year to those earning more than $301,000 : 40:1

Ratio of compensation paid AlliedSignal's CEO the year NAFTA went into effect to total wages the firm paid its 3,810 Mexican maquiladora workers : 3:2

Chance that a U.S. adult does not have a checking account : 1 in 5

Number of New York's East Harlem ATMs offering free service for the neighborhood's 11,000 welfare recipients in 1999 : 7

Number of the city's Upper East Side ATMs offering free service for the neighborhood's 700 welfare recipients that year : 120

Chance that an American declared bankruptcy in 1997 : 1 in 215

Chance that an American declared bankruptcy during the Depression : 1 in 215

Number of years Bob Dole's paternal grandparents lived off welfare : 6

Estimated number of assistance checks Dole officially signed for them as Kansas's Russell County Attorney : 60

Chance that a Republican man believes that "poor people have hard lives" : 1 in 5

Billions in new federal poverty spending that President Clinton proposed during his poverty tour in July 1999 : $1

Billions cut from the five-year federal food stamp budget in 1996 : $24

Year in which *Forbes* magazine stopped trying to count all the world's billionaires : 1997

Estimated gross global product per capita in the year 1000 : $133

Amount by which it had changed by the year 1700 : +$31

Estimated number of people today who live on less than $31 per month : 1,300,000,000

Estimated number who are enslaved : 27,000,000

Taxes

Maximum number of pages of tax forms an American was required to fill out in 1913 : 3

Number of pages of instructions provided : 1

Number of government entities in the U.S. that have the power to tax : 68,937

Ratio of the average amount a U.S. family spent on food, clothing, and shelter in 1999 to what it spent on taxes : 4:5

Ratio in 1968 : 5:4

Number of states in which the population's poorest fifth paid the largest portion of income in sales, property, and income taxes in 1997 : 40

Number of states in which two-parent families of four living at or below the federal poverty level are subject to income tax : 19

Percentage of Americans who believe that the U.S. tax code is not fair : 54

Estimated additional federal revenue that taxing corporations at 1951 rates would have generated in 1998 : +$122,800,000,000

Portion of IRS audits that are conducted on large corporations : $\frac{1}{500}$

Portion of fines levied and underpayments cited by the IRS each year for which large corporations are responsible : $\frac{1}{2}$

Average amount of U.S. taxes that multinational corporations have legally avoided paying each year since 1990 by using foreign accounts : $9,550,000,000

Value of the corporate tax breaks attached to the 1996 minimum-wage bill : $21,400,000,000

Percentage change in domestic discretionary spending required through 2002 to fund the tax cuts proposed by Congress in 1999 : –18

Portion of these tax cuts that would go to corporations : %10

Rank of the Manpower temporary agency among U.S. companies filing the largest number of W-2 forms each year : 1

Chance that an American earning more than $100,000 in 1988 was audited : 1 in 18

Chance that an American earning this much in 1996 was : 1 in 44

Percentage of the proceeds of the 1996 auction of Jacqueline Kennedy Onassis's effects that went for taxes : 75

Change since 1980 in the number of people who check the presidential-campaign-donation box on their tax forms : −10,500,000

Estimated minimum personal income tax that Steve Forbes would have saved in 1996 under the flat tax he advocated that year : $129,000

Projected cost of a poll that Newt Gingrich proposed in 1996 to assess Americans' view of the IRS : $35,000,000

IOUs

Estimated number of professional bounty hunters in the U.S. : 5,000

Percentage change since 1985 in the number of personal-bankruptcy applications filed in U.S. courts : +292

Estimated percentage change, since then, in the number of Americans undergoing credit counseling : +793

Estimated average amount Americans lose to securities fraud, per hour : $1,000,000

Number of S&Ls or shareholder groups seeking damages from the government over its handling of the 1980s bailout : 120

Estimated ratio of the awards sought to the bailout's original $165 billion cost : 1:5

Number of paragraphs of the 1999 federal budget devoted to passing the awards' costs on to taxpayers : 2

Percentage change since 1995 in the average late fee a credit card company charges : +90

Average number of months it takes an American to pay off holiday credit-card bills : 6

Number of years between 1950 and 1998 in which the U.S. Forest Service's timber program did not operate at a loss : 1

Amount oil companies owe the U.S. for undervaluing the oil pumped from public land between 1978 and 1997 : $2,050,000,000

Number of years a Texas senator prevented the government from charging market price : 2.5

Amount by which the U.N.'s estimate of what the U.S. owed it in dues in 1999 exceeded the Senate's estimate : $774,000,000

Portion of the U.N.'s 1998 debt accounted for by back dues owed by the U.S. : ⅔

Portion of total U.N. debt in 1998 accounted for by peace-keeping costs : ⅔

Ratio of the outstanding short-term debt that South Korea owed to foreign banks in 1997 to the size of the I.M.F.-led bailout that year : 1:1

Total bad debt Japan estimates was held by its banks in 1999, expressed as a percentage of GDP : 16.1

Total bad debt held by U.S. S&Ls in 1988, expressed as a percentage of U.S. GDP that year : 3.2

Number of countries whose "unsustainable" debt the World Bank identified as "in need" of relief in 1996 : 40

Number of these that had received debt relief two years later : 2

Estimated attendance at a rally advocating debt relief for poor countries held outside Britain's 1998 G-7 summit : 60,000

Percentage change in the size of the annual U.S. budget deficit during the Clinton Administration : –124

Ratio of federal spending on interest on the debt to spending on Medicare during the 1990s : 3:2

Amount that U.S. health-care professionals owed in defaulted student loans in 1998 : $107,000,000

Rank of chiropractors among those most likely to default : 1

Amount a London insurance firm will pay clients who can prove that they were impregnated by God : $1,500,000

Percentage of Americans who favor placing ads on the dollar bill to help cut the deficit or lower taxes : 35

Rolls of toilet paper received in lieu of an annual bonus in 1997 by each worker at a Moscow clock factory : 150

Number of days it took the workers to transport their bonuses home : 3

Imports and Exports

Ratio of Americans who opposed NAFTA's expansion in 1996 to those who voted for Bill Clinton that year : 3:1

Number of the sixty-five international trade disputes settled through the WTO that have resulted in a change in national policy or law : 59

Number of the ten trade disputes involving environmental or public-health issues that have resulted in a weakening of national laws : 10

Percentage of the twenty-four committee members advising the U.S. on WTO forest issues who are lumber executives : 100

Percentage change in Indonesia's paper-making capacity since 1995 : +200

Total U.S. arms sales to Indonesia since its 1975 invasion of East Timor : $1,200,000,000

Approximate year in which Asia had its first recorded trade deficit with Europe : 1835

Percentage change in the value of India's cotton exports between 1815 and 1832 : –92

Percentage change in the amount of British cotton products India imported during the same period : +1,500

Ratio of U.S. exports bought by mainland China in 1998 to those bought by Taiwan : 4:5

Value of U.S. export contracts signed by China during Jiang Zemin's first U.S. visit as premier in November 1997 : $4,260,000,000

Amount by which U.S. exports to China in 1997 fell short of U.S. exports to Belgium : $625,400,000

Rank of Indonesia, Belgium, and China among the top exporters of frog meat in 1999 : 1,2,3

Rank of Belgium among top exporters and importers of horse meat that year : 1

Ratio of the number of live turkeys imported to the U.S. in 1998 to the number exported : 3:2

Number of U.S. companies and groups licensed to sell merchandise bearing the Vatican's Jubilee 2000 logo : 31

Price a Paris boutique charges for 3.5 ounces of Yin Shen White Tea, "hand-picked by Chinese virgins" : $71.53

Average annual amount of U.S. chicken feet exported to China, in tons : 326,000

Price of a velvet-and-silk Chairman Mao jacket from Shanghai Tang, a boutique on New York's Madison Avenue : $670

Percentage change between 1996 and 1997 in Amway sales in China : +183

Chance that a Swiss army knife produced this year will be bought by the Swiss army : 1 in 700

Speculation

Portion of U.S. stock owned by the wealthiest 10 percent of Americans : $\frac{9}{10}$

Months before the 1929 stock market crash that *Forbes* magazine noted the "heroic scale" of U.S. economic growth : 4

Months' worth of salary lost by Groucho Marx in the crash : 28

Estimated amount lost by Isaac Newton on South Sea stock speculation in the 1720s : $2,000,000

Amount lost by Jack Kemp in the 1980s on his investment in a device purported to separate gold from sand : $50,000

Amount Comedy Central paid in May 1996 for two acres of Whitewater Development property : $10,000

Number of months later that the property was given away as part of a promotional campaign : 5

Change in the value of Ross Perot's portfolio on the day in February 1998 when one of his companies went public : +$882,112,600

Percentage change in the stock price of Microsoft rival Red Hat in the five weeks after the 1999 Microsoft antitrust ruling : +218

Ratio of Steven Jobs' earnings on the day his company's stock went public in 1995 to Michael Milken's earnings in 1987 : 1:1

Ratio of Jobs' average hourly earnings that day to the U.S. minimum wage : 13,421,052:1

Ratio of the average amount a white American spends on lottery tickets each year to what a black American spends : 1:5

Average amount Americans have spent on lottery tickets each day since 1995 : $94,552,000

Average amount Americans have contributed to the U.S. Treasury each day since then to help reduce the national debt : $8,096

Factor by which the average suicide rate in a U.S. city with legalized gambling exceeds that of a city without it : 2

Percentage change in the amount of presidential campaign contributions made by the gambling industry between 1992 and 1996 : +800

Percentage change in the population of Las Vegas since 1980 : +129

Estimated percentage return on investment that can be expected on the sale of cocaine smuggled into Miami : 300

Estimated percentage return on investment that can be expected on the sale of smuggled Freon : 1,200

Amount of the $5 billion that Exxon was ordered to pay in punitive damages in 1994 for the *Valdez* oil spill that it had paid by 1999 : 0

Estimated amount the company has earned by investing this money in the meantime : $5,000,000,000

Percentage return on its endowment that Harvard University would require in order to abolish tuition, according to a Harvard economist : 1.6

Total return on a dollar invested in the "socially responsible" Domini 400 Social Index in 1990 : $5.75

Total return on a dollar invested in the S&P 500 : $4.63

Number of nonbinding social-policy initiatives voted on by U.S. shareholders in 1997 and 1998 : 198

Number that passed : 0

Estimated factor by which U.S. stock market growth must exceed GDP for Social Security stock investment to work : 5

Number of years since 1900 in which this has occurred : 13

Number of heart attacks suffered on Wall Street the day the market dropped 513 points in 1998 : 2

Number suffered there the next day, when the market rose 288 points : 3

Chance that the Dow Jones Industrial Average reached a record high on any given trading day during the 1990s : 1 in 8

Length, in feet, of the longest soap bubble ever recorded : 105

The Corporate World

Chance that a U.S. corporate executive admits to spying on employees' e-mail : 1 in 3

Number of corporate spies in the Society of Competitive Intelligence Professionals : 6,600

Number of former U.S. representatives who are now Microsoft lobbyists : 4

Factor by which Microsoft's average monthly campaign contribution in 1999 exceeded its monthly contribution in 1995 : 8

Number of months between 1995 and 1996 that a Dow Chemical lobbyist on leave was a science fellow for the House Commerce Committee : 10

Weeks after the 1994 peso collapse that former Mexican President Carlos Salinas joined the board of Dow Jones : 4

Number of foreign lobbyists convicted since 1963 of failing to comply with U.S. financial-disclosure laws : 0

Ratio of the combined value of AOL and Time Warner on January 11, 2000, to the annual budget of France : 4:3

Severance pay received by Viacom CEO Frank Biondi after he was fired by the company in 1996 : $15,000,000

Severance pay Biondi received in 1998 after he was fired by Universal Pictures : $30,000,0000

Amount by which corporate funding for public radio in 1993 exceeded such funding in 1997 : $10,000

Percentage of all North American corporate sponsorship that goes to the arts : 6

Percentage that goes to sports : 67

Number of U.S. sports arenas named for corporations in 1999 : 17

Percentage change since 1990 in the number of prison beds in privately owned or managed U.S. prisons : +856

Purity of the gold that New York Life Insurance used in 1995 to gild its headquarters' dome, in karats : 22

Ratio of eToys' 1999 net sales through September to what it had spent by then on marketing and advertising : 2:3

Average percentage of revenue on a Wisconsin for-profit welfare agency's contract in 1999 that was profit : 17.1

Average percentage of revenue of a Fortune 500 company in 1999 that was profit : 5.3

Estimated portion of major U.S. companies downsized since 1990 whose profits have increased : ½

Number of lawsuits brought against the Cult Awareness Network by members of the Church of Scientology between 1991 and 1995 : 53

Number of months since the network went bankrupt and closed down in 1996 that Scientologists have owned and operated it : 37

Years a California rat retailer used the name Rats R Us before Toys 'R' Us threatened to sue : 2

Price charged for a "jumbo" rat by the rechristened Rat Paradise : $7.50

Amount that Nike has fruitlessly offered Ralph Nader to say "another shameless attempt by Nike to sell shoes" in a TV ad : $25,000

On the Job

Chance that a U.S. psychotherapist has a second job : 1 in 3

Rank of "office too cold" among white-collar employees' most common workplace complaints : 1

Rank of "office too hot" : 2

Amount the U.S. Treasury's Office of the Inspector General spent on a 1997 staff-morale study, per page : $4,538

Hourly fee paid the "ethics adviser" employed by Kenneth Starr during his first nineteen months as special prosecutor : $400

Fee for which The Amazing Kreskin offered to intercede in Starr's investigation of the president in 1998 : $1

Minimum income of a member of the U.S. lower middle class, as estimated in 1995 by North Carolina Representative Fred Heineman : $100,000

Chances that a U.S. worker's annual income fell short of this that year : 39 in 40

Amount the U.S. government spent between 1994 and 1999 to help U.S. workers laid off as a result of NAFTA : $152,000,000

Average amount paid each of the 211,582 workers approved for such aid : $718.40

Number of them who had been "indigenous crafts" workers in El Paso : 26

Rank of "foreign competition" among the causes of U.S. layoffs cited in 1996 by Americans not personally affected by them : 1

Rank of the country's "economic system" among the causes cited by those for whom layoffs have resulted in a "crisis" : 1

Number of Americans employed domestically by U.S. subsidiaries of foreign corporations in 1998 : 5,000,000

Average percentage change in the salary of an American who changed jobs during the 1990–92 recession : –22

Average figure given by Americans in 1996 when asked to estimate what percentage of the population was unemployed : 20.6

Percentage of Americans who were actually unemployed that year : 5.2

Chance that an unemployed U.S. worker receives unemployment benefits : 1 in 3

Average percentage of job cuts each year since 1995 that resulted from mergers or acquisitions : 11

Chance that a federal job-training program in the early 1990s kept records of its clients' placement rates : 1 in 2

Federal payments made in 1994 to government employees who resigned as part of a downsizing program : $912,000,000

Federal salaries paid that year to newly hired government employees : $780,689,202

Percentage change during the Nineties in the number of Americans employed by the federal government : −13

Percentage change in the number employed by state governments : +15

Ratio of U.S. workers earning the minimum wage to those earning less : 1:2

Chances that a minimum-wage earner is over the age of nineteen : 2 in 3

Percentage by which 1998's minimum wage would have been increased if its growth since 1968 had kept pace with inflation : 34

Number of cities that required companies receiving public funds to pay a "living wage" above the federal legal minimum in 1998 : 11

Rank of 1953 among years in which the largest percentage of U.S. workers were unionized : 1

Chances that a Disney World employee is : 2 in 5

Rank of Disney World among the country's largest single-site employers : 1

Percentage change since 1970 in the number of Americans employed by U.S. toy manufacturers : −54

Percentage of U.S. artists who earn less than $3,000 a year for their art : 45

Number of National Public Radio employees whose salaries exceed $100,000 : 19

Number of Department of Veterans Affairs employees whose salaries exceed this : 9,173

Number of Americans employed by Wal-Mart for every resident of North Dakota : 1.2

Number of hairstylists for every teacher in Detroit : 0.7

Hours of training required to become a licensed hair braider in the state of New York : 900

Hours of training required to become a New York State emergency medical technician : 136

Number of former welfare recipients that New York City trained in 1999 to work as phone psychics : 15

Number of Americans now employed as "serfs" or "wenches" at Medieval Times entertainment complexes in the U.S. : 1,400

Number of weeks in 1972 during which Bill Gates served as a congressional page : 8

Shopping

Number of Mighty Moms and Dedicated Dads employed by Minnesota's Mall of America to confront rowdy teens with "verbal judo" : 20

Percentage change between 1988 and 1997 in the average amount U.S. grandparents say they spend annually on their grandchildren : +50

Price of a sheet of "undipped" blotter-acid paper signed by Timothy Leary, from San Francisco's ArtRock Gallery : $475

Year in which Mattel sold its last Pilgrim Barbie : 1995

Percentage of the U.S. retail price of a pair of Pocahontas pajamas in 1996 that was paid to the Haitian who sewed them : 0.06

Amount Americans spend each day on goods produced by prison labor : $4,297,000

Ratio of Kmart's U.S. sales in 1998 to the estimated budget of the Russian military : 1:1

Price McDonnell Douglas charged the U.S. Air Force in 1995 for each C-17 airplane hinge delivered : $2,187

Price per hinge the company had originally charged before replacing a subcontractor it considered "too slow" : $30

Price of *Well . . . There You Go Again*, a 1996 CD-ROM collection of the witticisms of Ronald Reagan : $49.95

Price paid in 1995 for a White House telephone used during the Nixon Administration : $600

Price paid in 1998 for the ambulance that carried Lee Harvey Oswald after he was shot by Jack Ruby, original stretcher and oxygen tanks included : $40,000

Portion of Abraham Zapruder's initial profits from his footage of JFK's assassination that he reported to the Warren Commission in 1964 : ½

Average amount an American earning at least $250,000 in 1998 said that he or she would be willing to pay to become president : $55,000

Average amount that he or she would be willing to pay to find "true love" : $487,000

Legal fees paid by Princess Diana's memorial fund in 1999 to stop the Franklin Mint's sale of Diana souvenirs : $48,000

Amount that Florida governor Jeb Bush's wife spent on a five-day shopping trip to Paris in 1998 : $19,000

Amount she declared to U.S. Customs : $500

Chance that a pair of women's shoes sold in the U.S. is sold by Nine West : 1 in 5

Price of a pair of earrings shaped like the atomic bombs dropped on Japan, from the U.S. Atomic Museum gift shop : $20

Number of jars of Exxon *Valdez* oil sludge sold by the state of Alaska since November, 1997, to help pay cleanup costs : 2,000

Percentage of Americans polled in the first week of December 1999 who said they had never made a purchase over the Internet : 70

Percentage of Americans who believe that "most of us buy and consume more than we need" : 82

SCIENCE

Technology

Outer Space

Weather Conditions

Reaping and Sowing

The Animal Kingdom

The Environment

Energy

Genetics

Health Risks

Health Care

Epidemics

Technology

World's record speed, in miles per hour, of a walking robot : 13

Number of voice commands a 1999 Jaguar S-Type sedan understands : 44

Average amount by which the use of a seat belt decreases an auto-accident victim's hospital bills : $5,000

Number of titles for "horseless carriages" issued to new car owners in Maine in the spring of 1999 due to a Y2K error : 2,000

Gallons of untreated sewage that spilled onto L.A.'s streets in June 1999 after a sanitation plant's Y2K test : 1,200,000

Chance that an IBM-compatible personal computer made since 1997 contained Y2K flaws : 1 in 2

Number of countries that had not made public their assessment of the Y2K readiness of their computer systems by October 1999 : 91

Portion of the Defense Department's "mission critical" computer systems that were found to be vulnerable to the Y2K bug in June 1999 : $\frac{1}{10}$

Portion of all research time on government supercomputers granted in 1996 that went to military scientists : $\frac{1}{2}$

Estimated portion that went to military scientists in 1998 : $\frac{5}{6}$

Year in which the U.S. military began using video games to train soldiers to kill : 1989

Ratio of applicants to slots in 1998 for DigiPen Institute's degree program in video-game design and computer animation : 10:1

Chance that an American believes "100 computers could solve our country's problems better than 100 politicians" : 1 in 3

Seconds of booing elicited by Steven Jobs' announcement of Apple's software development deal with Microsoft at a 1997 trade show : 42

Ratio of decibels emitted by an airplane's jet engine to those emitted by "the Trap," a car alarm : 1:1

Price for which Britain's Avon Silversmiths offered a gold-plated crucifix pendant with a built-in alarm in 1998 : $414

Number of registered patents for golf-related inventions : 13,665

Number for bowling-related inventions : 570

Number of years between the invention of photocopier technology in 1938 and the first commercial-copier sale : 21

Average annual number of copies produced per Amercan six years later : 52

Patent number awarded Abraham Lincoln in 1849 on a device for "buoying vessels over shoals" : 6,469

Outer Space

"Symbolic portion" of Gene Roddenberry and Timothy Leary shot into orbit in 1996, in ounces of ashes apiece : 0.25

Percentage of the 8,658 man-made objects orbiting the Earth that have been classified as "debris" : 69

Estimated ratio of satellites in the path of 1998's Leonid meteor shower to those in the path of the previous one in 1966 : 10:1

Number of meteors entering the Earth's atmosphere each year that are larger than an automobile : 12

Estimated average number of Martian rocks that land on Earth each month : 4

Pounds of sunlight that hit the Earth each second : 4.3

Seconds by which a "slingshot" maneuver performed by a NASA probe in August 1999 slowed the Earth's rotation : 10^{-12}

Chance that a U.S. adult knows how long it takes the Earth to orbit the sun : 1 in 2

Number of academic chairs worldwide devoted to the search for extraterrestrial intelligence : 1

Percentage of Americans who believe they have seen a UFO : 11

Ratio of TV viewers who watched a 1973 Elvis Presley concert to those who watched the 1969 moon landing : 3:1

Percentage of Canadian adults under the age of twenty-five who believe that Neil Armstrong was the first Canadian in space : 10

Number of the three John Glenn action figures introduced in 1998 that are dressed in a suit and tie : 1

Number of people who have been to space : 390

Number of minor planets named after rock musicians : 13

Number of Wal-Mart plastic owls that a NASA employee bought in 1994 to protect the space shuttle from woodpeckers : 6

Number of days that an unauthorized visitor spent undetected at a NASA mission control console during a 1997 shuttle mission : 2

Average number of times each day that NASA's computers accessed the *Penthouse* Web site in 1995 : 153

Amount by which NASA is over budget in its spending on the international space station : $6,000,000,000

Change since 1996 in the estimated number of galaxies observable from Earth : +125,000,000,000

Factor by which the estimated size of the universe has been increased since 1900 : 1,000,000

Number of the universe's spatial dimensions of which physicists now believe we are unaware : 7

Weather Conditions

Chance that an American is "really intrigued by the underlying causes of bad weather" : 1 in 2

Chances that a Briton is : 2 in 3

Price charged by the Weather Channel in 1996 for *Forecast for Victory*, a video exploring weather's "intriguing role" in World War II : $19.95

Ratio of rainfall during the 1995–96 drought in the U.S. winter-wheat belt to rainfall there during the height of the Dust Bowl : 2:3

Percentage by which drought conditions reduced the level of the Potomac River between 1998 and 1999 : 60

Number of years since 1988 in which natural disasters have cost U.S. insurers at least $1 billion : 12

Number of years prior to 1988 in which this occurred : 0

Percentage change since 1960 in the number of Americans living in the four states most prone to natural disasters : +109

Rank of Chicago, among windiest U.S. cities : 53

Rank of Dodge City, Kansas : 1

Average percentage by which the amount of East Coast rainfall on a Saturday exceeds the amount on a Monday : 22

Average percentage by which East Coast air pollution levels on Thursday exceed those on Monday : 24

Estimated temperature of hell, according to two Spanish physicists' interpretation of the Bible : 832°F

Estimated temperature of heaven : 448°F

Number of months between May 1997 and August 1998 that did not break a record for average global heat : 0

Estimated number of calls made to Californian Al Niño between 1997 and 1998 by people asking, "Why are you doing this?" : 100

Milliseconds by which El Niño's drag on the Earth's rotation extended an average day's length in 1997 : .04

Average amount insurers paid to victims of climate-related disasters each day during the 1980s, worldwide : $8,000,000

Average amount paid such victims each day during the 1990s : $23,500,000

Number of British women killed in 1999 by lightning conducted through their underwire bras : 2

Ratio of April showers to plants that produced May flowers at the Springfield, Illinois, Park District in 1999 : 1:1,571

Rank of April among the cruelest months : 1

Reaping and Sowing

Estimated number of acres of U.S. farmland lost to development each hour : 114

Percentage change since 1997 in direct government payment to U.S. farmers : +200

Percentage change since then in total farm income, including government payments : −1

Annual amount the U.S. government spends to maintain a one-acre medicinal-marijuana farm in Mississippi : $250,000

Rank of China among the world's largest tobacco producers : 1

Rank of chemical fertilizer among the top agricultural products the U.S. exported to China in 1999 : 1

Maximum tonnage by which pollution reduced China's potential annual wheat production between 1994 and 1996 : 10,000

Tons of wheat China imported during this period : 10,000

Number of millennia before humans first farmed that farmer ants were farming the spongy fungus on which they feed : 50,000

Estimated bushels of maize paid annually to the Aztec rulers of the city of Tenochtitlán by their subjects : 210,000

Inches by which today's largest corncobs exceed the length of those grown in Mexico in 1500 : 12

Number of *Crocus sativus* flowers required to produce one pound of saffron : 68,182

Maximum ratio of curvature to length allowed a Grade 1 cucumber under the European Union's 1998 produce regulations : 1:10

Pounds of manure a French farmers' association dumped in front of a McDonald's in Arles, France, in August 1999 : 2,000

Year in which Britain's Prince Charles began farming organically : 1986

Rank of broccoli and peaches, respectively, among U.S.-grown produce with the highest residual pesticide levels : 18,1

Number of insect species worldwide that are known to be pesticide-resistant : 533

Percentage change between 1996 and 1998 in the acres of U.S. cropland planted with genetically engineered crops : +866

Percentage of the Fall 1998 issue of Britain's *The Ecologist* magazine devoted to an investigation of Monsanto : 95

Percentage of the issue's entire press run that was immediately pulped by the printer, for fear of breaking British libel laws : 100

Number of times in 1997 that a Florida Fox-TV station asked two reporters to rewrite a news story on Monsanto : 83

Amount the station offered the reporters to quit their jobs and keep silent after the news story was killed : $151,250

Average number of peas in a pod : 8

The Animal Kingdom

Number of Washington, D.C., cherry trees felled in the spring of 1999 by beavers : 4

Number of wild turkeys in New Hampshire in 1968 : 0

Number there today : 10,000

Percentage change since 1940 in the state's black bear population : +375

Percentage change since the 1970s in the number of salmon in the Atlantic Ocean : –90

Ratio of the number of chickens sold at U.S. KFCs each day to the number killed in the January 1998 Hong Kong flu scare : 3:2

Days of prayer that Buddhist monks and nuns in Hong Kong devoted to the souls of slaughtered chickens that winter : 7

Number of Thanksgiving turkeys granted a presidential pardon since 1947 : 53

Fine levied on a California man in 1999 for shooting an owl out of a tree with a slingshot and beating it with a board : $10,000

Chance that a Mexican gray wolf released into the Arizona wilderness in the spring of 1998 had been shot by that November : 1 in 2

Percentage of European rabbits in southern Australia killed in 1995 by the inadvertent release of a virus : 95

Percentage that the virus's planned release was meant to kill : 100

Percentage of New England's feral honeybee population lost to Asian mites since 1995 : 98

Portion of Yellowstone National Park's bison herd killed after straying beyond park boundaries in 1997 : ½

Percentage of all privately owned bison in the U.S. that belong to Ted Turner : 7

Percentage change between 1994 and 1998 in membership in the American Emu Association : –70

Number of people who have been killed by captive elephants in the U.S. since 1983 : 17

Average number of times a U.S. beekeeper is stung each year : 400

Average number of mosquitoes a dragonfly consumes each day : 300

Maximum number to which rats have been trained to count : 45

Number of elephants enrolled in painting schools in Thailand : 10

Estimated number of robins that mistake electric light for dawn each night in Great Britain : 10,000

Estimated percentage change since 1979 in the number of birds killed annually by U.S. communications towers : +186

Number of the twenty-three species seriously depleted by the 1989 Exxon *Valdez* spill that recovered : 2

Maximum number of months humanity could survive without invertebrates : 6

Percentage of the lab animals launched aboard NASA's Neurolab in 1998 that died in orbit, snails excluded : 70

Number of animals that died in accidents at Disney's Animal Kingdom park before it opened in 1998 : 27

Combined number of root canals performed since 1996 on two Kodiak bears at the San Francisco Zoo : 11

Portion of Tanzania's lion population lost to canine distemper in 1994 : ⅓

Percentage of Hawaiian bird species that have become extinct since 1778 : 49

Number of colonies of Antarctic Adélie penguins that have disappeared since 1988 : 11

Age at death in 1998 of the sturgeon, Nikita, Khrushchev's 1964 gift to Norway, after an accidental immersion in saltwater : 38

Number of live contraband Chinese chipmunks that the Dutch government ordered KLM airlines to shred in April 1999 : 440

Number of North America's six sea turtle species that are not endangered : 1

Number of dodo heads successfully preserved since the bird's extinction in 1638 : 1

The Environment

Number of oil spills larger than that of the Exxon *Valdez* that have occurred since 1989 : 10

Ratio of the amount of oil spilled by the Exxon *Valdez* to that spilled during the Gulf War : 1:24

Ratio of the amount of oil spilled by the Exxon *Valdez* to the amount of oil spilled into the Mediterranean Sea each year : 1:17

Percentage change in the number of British ponds since 1900 : −75

Minimum number of miles of West Virginia streams buried by mining waste since 1986 : 470

Estimated number of centimeters by which the angle of the Earth's axis has shifted since 1950 due to dam-related water distribution : 60

Estimated number of miles by which the Earth's ionosphere has dropped since 1958 : 5

Number of feet by which Arctic Sea ice has thinned since 1976 : 4

Size of an iceberg that separated from Antarctica in January 1995, in ice cubes : 70,000,000,000,000,000

Size of an iceberg that separated in October 1998, in square yards : 6,300,000,000

Number of inches it would sink if every person on the planet had stood on it : 2

Square miles of errant Antarctic icebergs being tracked by the National Ice Center in Washington, D.C. : 10,000

Percentage increase in the ozone gap over Antarctica since 1997 : 37

Square miles by which the size of the ozone hole exceeds the size of North America : 1,129,000

Ratio of the size of Lake Ontario to the size of the Gulf of Mexico's polluted "dead zone" : 1:1

Estimated increase in underwater ocean noise between 1989 and 1999, in decibels : 6.5

Estimated percentage of coral reefs in the Indian Ocean that were killed by rising sea temperatures in 1998 : 99

Number of U.S. Army tanks the Army Corps of Engineers "deployed" off Alabama's coast in 1994 to create a reef : 100

Number of tires found along the Mississippi River since 1997 by an Illinois man bent on cleaning it : 1,916

Average amount of trash generated by a Super Bowl game, in tons : 70

Percentage that is later reused or recycled : 7

Number of the ten billion plastic Coke bottles distributed in the U.S. each year that are made from recycled material : 0

Average number of acres of Arizona's Sonora Desert that are "developed" each day : 24

Acres of old-growth forest that Wilderness Society president John Roush had cleared from his ranch in 1995 : 65

Portion of Texas industrial plants operating under "grand-fathered" emissions rules that predate the state's 1971 Clean Air Act : ½

Percentage of California counties declared disaster areas in February 1998 : 60

Annual cost of containing plants and animals accidentally irra-diated at Washington's Hanford Nuclear Site : $2,000,000

Number of U.S. representatives cited as "environmental zeroes" in 1998 by the League of Conservation Voters : 41

Energy

Ratio of the price of a gallon of crude oil to the wholesale price of a gallon of Evian water in January 1999 : 1:11

Ratio of RAM needed to run the space shuttle's onboard computers in 1998 to that needed to run WordPerfect for Windows 95 : 5:8

Chances that a computer is left on overnight : 2 in 5

Estimated amount spent each year on electricity to operate all the exit signs in U.S. buildings : $1,000,000,000

Chance that a kilowatt hour of electricity used in the U.S. in 1998 was generated from a renewable resource : 1 in 9

Percentage change in U.S. power-company investments in energy efficiency programs since restructuring of the utility industry began in 1994 : –45

Megawatts by which the world's nuclear-power capacity changed during 1998 : –230

Megawatts by which the world's wind-power capacity changed that year : +2,200

Pounds of plutonium that a British nuclear plant has dumped into the Irish Sea since 1959 : 397

Days after Ukraine reopened a nuclear reactor at Chernobyl in November 1999 that a water leak forced a shutdown : 6

Percentage of federal nuclear-safety inspectors that the Senate proposed laying off in 1998 : 37

Percentage of U.S. nuclear reactors that have reported safety violations since 1996 : 91

Chance that a U.S. nuclear power plant's indoor waste-storage facility is full : 1 in 5

Truckloads of nuclear waste the Department of Energy began driving to New Mexico for storage in 1999 : 38,000

Number of highway accidents the DOE estimates that these shipments will be involved in through the year 2034 : 50

Estimated gallons of gasoline wasted in U.S. traffic jams each day : 27,000,000

Number of super tankers it would take to hold the gas wasted this way each year : 134

Estimated gallons of jet fuel required to send Al Gore to Kyoto's Global Warming Conference in December 1997 : 60,000

Gallons of oil leaked into the Gulf of Mexico this year after an oil rig's anchor punctured an underwater pipeline : 94,500

Estimated tons of PCBs that General Electric has leaked into the Hudson River since 1977's ban on dumping the toxin : 6.8

Ratio of the voltage of fences at two of Alabama's high-security prisons to that of an electric chair : 7:2

Seconds after the fence is touched that it resets to a lethal charge : 0.25

Number of years that Secretary of Energy Hazel O'Leary used an electric spaceheater in her DOE office : 4

Number of years beyond which only someone "probably certifiable" would head the DOE, according to O'Leary : 4

Genetics

Percentage by which the estimate of the number of genes on the human genome has increased since 1995 : 100

Percentage change since 1994 in the number of mice genetically engineered to exhibit a human disease : +900

Weeks after DNA testing revealed Bill Clinton's sexual dalliance in 1999 that such testing revealed Thomas Jefferson's as well : 7

Chance, according to the Starr Report, that the semen on Monica Lewinsky's dress was not that of President Clinton : 1 in 7,870,000,000,000

Percentage of Iceland's gene pool to which Decode Genetics acquired exclusive commercial rights in January 2000 : 100

Daily number of Icelanders who opted to exclude their health records from Decode's national database over the following month : 100

Percentage of Iceland's total population that had opted out by then : 7

Number of forty-foot refrigerated biological-evidence trailers used by the LAPD : 4

Fee that an anonymous family has paid Texas A&M University to clone their pet collie-mix, Missy : $2,300,000

Price a Houston company charged in 1998 for sending a DNA sample into outer space for possible cloning by aliens : $50

Percentage change in the losses of PPL Therapeutics, the Scottish biotechnology company, in the two years after it cloned Dolly, the world's first cloned sheep : +40

Number of days in 1998 that a British art museum exhibited a mound of Dolly's dung : 51

Percentage of Americans who say they would not enjoy spending time with their own clone : 70

Percentage of Americans who believe that "everyone is their own god" : 3

Chance that a U.S. parent would abort a baby predisposed to obesity : 1 in 9

Health Risks

Year in which, at the current rate of increase, all Americans will be overweight : 2075

Average amount of pressure a U.S. woman exerts on a stiletto heel, in pounds per square inch : 552

Factor by which "a cynical view" and "aggressive responses to stress" may increase arterial calcium deposits : 2

Chance that a police officer killed in the line of duty between 1985 and 1996 was shot with his own gun : 1 in 6

Estimated portion of annual spending on the treatment of gunshot wounds that comes from the federal government : ½

Ratio of Americans who are murdered each year to the number who die from tobacco-related illnesses : 1:17

Percentage of Americans who have never smoked who say that tobacco companies are to blame for smoking-related illnesses : 22

Percentage of American smokers who say this : 13

Percentage change between 1996 and 1997 in the number of U.S. senators and representatives who admit to being smokers : −22

Ratio of the number of days the 105th Senate devoted to hearings on presidential scandals to those it spent debating Medicaid or Medicare : 3:2

Amount by which Medicare's outlays exceeded contributions in 1995, the first year the program had a deficit : $36,000,000

Size of the Medicare deficit one year later : $4,200,000,000

Percentage of elderly Medicare patients in fee-for-service plans whose health declined during a four-year study : 28

Percentage of elderly Medicare patients in HMOs whose health declined : 54

Ratio of the number of OB-GYNs over the age of sixty-four who perform abortions to those under the age of forty who do : 4:3

Chances that an OB-GYN who performs abortions is over the age of fifty : 3 in 5

Factor by which women over the age of sixty who smoke are more likely to develop lung cancer than men of the same age who smoke : 2

Percentage change since 1930 in the annual number of cancer deaths per 1,000 people : +11

Percentage change since then in the number of cancer deaths per 1,000 people, excluding lung cancer : −20

Estimated chances that a U.S. child diagnosed with leukemia will be in remission five years later : 4 in 5

Estimated chances that an Iraqi child diagnosed with leukemia will live that long : 0

Number of Sudanese factories besides the one bombed by the U.S. in 1998 that had U.N. approval to export drugs to Iraq : 0

Estimated portion of all medicinal drugs introduced since 1980 that are unavailable in Cuba due to the U.S. embargo : ½

Number of the 148 U.S. polio cases reported between 1980 and 1997 that were caused by the vaccine itself : 140

Chance that an American who contracted rabies from bats since 1981 survived the illness : 0

Chance that the victim noticed being bitten : 1 in 20

Average number of dog bites sustained by Americans each day : 12,877

Average daily amount U.S. insurers pay to cover them : $2,739,726

Number of emergency-room visits for electric-fan-related injuries in 1997 : 16,073

Number of hospital warehouse fires in 1995 attributed to the spontaneous combustion of latex patient-examination gloves : 4

Dimensions, in inches, of a gauze pad left in an Iowa man during a 1994 operation : 14 x 14

Percentage of doctors in intensive-care units in the U.S. who wash their hands appropriately, according to a 1999 study : 17

Average annual number of Americans who pick up new infections while hospitalized : 2,000,000

Factor by which fake fingernails increase the likelihood that a health-care worker's fingers carry infectious bacteria even after hand washing : 1.6

Chances that a nurse would not want a relative to be treated in the hospital where he or she works : 2 in 5

Estimated number of Americans who regain consciousness during surgery each year : 40,000

Health Care

Average number of seconds a U.S. patient is allowed to speak before being interrupted by a doctor : 18

Chance that a person diagnosed with high blood pressure presents normal pressure when not at the doctor's office : 1 in 4

Chance that a Florida rape victim's account will be believed by hospital medical personnel : 1 in 2

Chances that a U.S. Catholic hospital does not provide emergency contraception to rape victims : 4 in 5

Portion of fee-for-service health insurance plans in 1988 whose prescription coverage included oral contraceptives : 1 in 3

Last year in which the majority of U.S. OB-GYN residents were men : 1991

Average percentage by which a U.S. woman's out-of-pocket medical expenses exceeded those of a U.S. man in 1998 : 68

Percentage by which HMO Kaiser Permanente estimated in 1998 that covering Viagra would drive up its pharmacy costs : 10

Percentage by which it actually did : 1

Number of bills proposing HMO regulations introduced in state legislatures in 1997 : 1,200

Change since 1987 in a U.S. household's average spending on medical services, supplies, and drugs : –$99.69

Change since then in a household's annual spending on health insurance : +$323.28

Net change in the number of Americans who have lost their health insurance each month since 1996 : +125,000

Chance that an American without health insurance earns at least $50,000 per year : 1 in 4

Estimated percentage of U.S. hospital deaths that follow a decision to withhold treatment : 70

Chance that a patient on the national waiting list for an organ will receive one this year : 1 in 3

Year in which Kalawo, Hawaii, the U.S. county with the largest income gap, ceased functioning as a leper colony : 1969

Year that Hawaii outlawed use of the word "leprosy" : 1949

Hours of charity work performed monthly by doctors who receive more than 85 percent of their income from managed care : 5

Hours performed by doctors who receive no money from managed care : 10

Chances that a managed-care patient is unaware of being enrolled in managed care : 2 in 3

Yards by which a failed suicide missed a rowboating psychiatrist after jumping off the San Francisco Bay Bridge in 1995 : 6

Epidemics

Chance that a fourteenth-century European was killed by bubonic plague : 1 in 4

Chance that a sixteenth-century Aztec was killed by smallpox : 1 in 2

Year in which the *New York Times* first reported a "Rare Cancer Seen in 41 Homosexuals" : 1981

Chance that a San Francisco AIDS doctor has helped at least one patient commit suicide : 1 in 2

Chance that a U.S. adult has suffered from some form of post-traumatic stress disorder : 1 in 13

Average amount Americans spend on legal drugs per second : $2,600

Estimated retail price of one year of AIDS drugs in South Africa in 1999, expressed as a percentage of per capita GDP : 188

Estimated amount that South Africa's national health-care plan could save if the AIDS drug AZT were domestically man-ufactured : $987,000,000

Percentage by which the U.N. reported in 1997 that it had underestimated the number of new HIV infections in the pre-vious year : 41

Percentage change between 1980 and 1992 in the number of HIV-negative Americans who died of infectious diseases : +56

Number of cases of smallpox that the World Health Organization considers a "global emergency" : 1

Percentage change between 1997 and 1998 in the number of cholera cases worldwide : +99

Factor by which Africa's cholera fatality rate exceeds the rate achievable with proper treatment and adequate sanitation : 5

Number of Africans used to test a U.S. polio vaccine made with primate kidney cells in the 1950s : 1,000,000

Number of the forty-six Africans found to be HIV-positive before 1981 who lived within ninety miles of the vaccine trials : 45

Estimated percentage of all AIDS deaths since 1980 that took place in Africa : 83

Average number of Zimbabweans killed by AIDS each week in 1999 : 2,500

Average number of school teachers in Cote d'Ivoire killed by AIDS each school day : 1

Chances that a child orphaned by AIDS lives in Africa : 19 in 20

Projected age to which the AIDS epidemic will lower the life expectancy in sub-Saharan Africa by 2000 : 45

PSYCHOLOGY

Anxiety

Narcissism

Fears

Beliefs

Anxiety

Chance that an American reports being shy : 1 in 2

Chance that a U.S. adult under the age of fifty-four suffers from mental-health and/or substance-abuse problems : 1 in 3

Change between 1994 and 1996 in the number of antidepressant prescriptions filled each day for managed-care patients : +34,542

Projected rank of heart disease and severe depression among the leading causes of death and disability in 2020 : 1,2

Ratio of Americans who said in 1995 that they worried "a lot" about money and health insurance to those who said they worried about going to hell : 5:1

Percentage of Americans who believed in 1995 that citizens do not have the right to buy and store "large quantities of weapons" : 71

Percentage who said that armed, antigovernment groups should be infiltrated "even if it infringes on their constitutional rights" : 72

Chance that a U.S. adult in 1994 believed that "the next generation will enjoy less personal freedom" : 1 in 2

Chance that an applicant to a U.S. police force in 1992 was found to be "overly aggressive" based on psychological tests : 1 in 2

Number of suicide notes found in a North Carolina inmate's cell the day before his scheduled execution in 1997 : 2

Hours before the scheduled execution that he was granted an indefinite stay for "psychiatric evaluation" : 16

Price per minute that a San Francisco hotel charges guests for a phone session with its on-call psychologist : $2

Number of seconds that the average American can wait for an elevator before becoming visibly agitated : 40

Chance that an American would prefer to spend more time alone : 1 in 3

Narcissism

Number of times California has prosecuted Ubiquitous Perpetuity God, formerly Enrique Silberg, for indecent exposure : 3

Percentage of Americans who said in 1994 that their financial situation was "at least somewhat" reflective of "God's regard" for them : 70

Number of virgins who bought a London insurance company's policy against giving birth "by act of God" in the year 2000 : 4,812

Ratio of the circulation of *Weight Watchers Magazine* to that of the *New York Times* : 1:1

Percentage of the 2.3 million gallons of blood Americans could donate each month that they actually do : 0.1

Percentage change in the daily number of queries regarding burial at sea received by the Navy in the month following the death of John F. Kennedy Jr. in 1999 : +250

Ratio of Americans applying to be on MTV's *The Real World* in 1998 to those applying to the Peace Corps that year : 5:2

Percentage of Americans who believe that Bill Clinton should see a therapist : 44

Number of times Bob Dole said "Bob Dole" during a 1996 speech to the Iowa Pork Producers Association : 12

Rank of "listening to other students" among the classroom activities that schoolchildren find the most boring : 1

Fears

Number of bulletproof Bibles manufactured in 1996 by California's Innovative Marketing Alliance : 1,000

Chance that an American believes that a man-made disaster will destroy civilization in the twenty-first century : 1 in 2

Percentage change since 1993 in the number of exorcists appointed by Catholic bishops nationwide : +900

Chances that a U.S. doctor specializing in pain has withheld medication out of fear of losing his or her license : 2 in 5

Number of Baltimore city blocks under twenty-four-hour video surveillance by local police in 1996 : 16

Number in 1999 : 32

Number of microphones installed in Redwood City, California, in 1996 as part of "Shot Spotter," an "urban gunfire location system" : 8

Number of town residents killed by random gunfire before the program was instituted : 0

Estimated number of Americans who belong to a neighborhood crime-watch program : 17,000,000

Price of a database assessing current and future crime risks for any location in the U.S., from CAP Index : $35,000

Chance that an American would rather be mugged than audited : 1 in 2

Percentage of Americans earning more than $60,000 who believe "the meek shall inherit the earth" : 36

Number of New York City children who had been issued Civil Defense dog tags by 1952 as a means of identifying them after a nuclear attack : 2,500,000

Percentage change between 1969 and 1998 in the annual number of planes hijacked worldwide : −89

Percentage change since 1987 in the number of terrorist incidents : −59

Chance that an act of terrorism killed an American in the 1980s : 1 in 9

Chance of this in the Nineties : 1 in 50

Beliefs

Estimated size of heaven, in cubic miles, according to the Reverend Billy Graham : 1,500

Rank of "enemies" and the President, among the people most often prayed for in 1998 by Americans who said they prayed : 4,5

Annual donation to the Salesian Sisters of St. John Bosco that will reserve a place in one of their nuns' daily prayers : $100

Percentage of Americans who believe that Jesus Christ sinned during his lifetime : 42

Chance that an American believes that Joan of Arc was Noah's wife : 1 in 8

Chance that a resident of France said in 1994 that believing in God was no longer "necessary" : 1 in 3

Estimated percentage increase since 1000 in the world's Christian, Muslim, and Hindu populations, respectively : 2,450, 2,300, 1,025

Estimated percentage increase in the Buddhist population : 4,275

Percentage of those attending 1997's International Summer Institute for Youth in Holocaust Studies camp in Vermont who were Jewish : 8

Number of Jewish Holocaust victims baptized posthumously into the Mormon Church without survivors' permission before the practice ended in 1995 : 380,000

Number of Salt Lake City residents who converted to Southern Baptism during a one-week evangelism drive in 1998 : 1,717

Chance that an American believes that the government is concealing evidence of alien visitations : 1 in 2

Percentage of Americans who said in 1998 they were confident that passenger trips to the moon would occur in their lifetime : 29

Percentage who said they were confident that Social Security would provide them with "significant" income : 26

Chance that a House member voted in favor of a 1998 constitutional amendment allowing school prayer : 1 in 2

Chance that a member attended Congress's opening daily prayer on any of the three days preceding the vote : 1 in 29

Chance that an American believes that Bill Clinton is "a bigger threat to the American way of life" than Saddam Hussein : 1 in 5

Percentage of Americans who say that "government" is the biggest obstacle to middle-class prosperity : 28

Percentage who say that "corporate greed" is : 46

Months after Martin Luther King Jr. publicly called the U.S. the "world's greatest purveyor of violence" that he was killed : 2

Days after a baby was stolen from a murdered woman's womb in 1995 that Newt Gingrich blamed "the welfare state" : 4

Chance that an American who believes that abortion is murder also believes that it is "sometimes the best course" : 1 in 3

Estimated number of abortions performed on born-again or Evangelical Christians each year in the U.S. : 258,000

Chance that an American believes that "most people can be trusted" : 1 in 3

Year in which current ideas of normalcy may be seen as "pathology," according to a U.S. pharmaceutical executive in 1997 : 2016

Portion of the world's population that he believes might then be prescribed psychiatric drugs : ⅓

Percentage of Americans earning less than $30,000 a year who believe "the meek shall inherit the earth" : 61

Percentage change since 1916 in the number of U.S. scientists who say they believe in a god : 0

HOME EC

Married Life

Modern Baby Making

Family Affairs

Around the House

Edibles and Potables

Shelter

Married Life

Chance that a romance cited by *People* magazine in 1996 as among the century's "greatest love stories" was adulterous : 1 in 2

Height, in feet, of a scarlet "A" with which a Washington woman marked her family's yard in 1998 to protest her father's adultery : 7

Percentage of Americans who said in 1996 that "adultery can sometimes be good for a marriage" : 22

Percentage who said in 1994 that they would allow their spouse to have sex with a stranger in exchange for $1 million : 10

Ratio of husbands who say they fell in love with their spouse at first sight to wives who say this : 2:1

Percentage of newlyweds who say they consummated their relationship on the first date : 17

Last year in which it was legal to marry a fourteen-year-old in Utah : 1999

Number of years that a Utah man had been married before discovering in 1995 that his wife was not a woman : 3.5

Percentage of the funds spent fighting Alaska's gay-marriage initiative in 1998 that came from the Mormon Church : 79

Estimated number of married Episcopalian clergymen ordained as Catholic priests in the U.S. since 1981 : 112

Percentage change since 1974 in the number of annulments granted to Catholic couples in the U.S. : +174

Number of GOP representatives who voted for 1996's Defense of Marriage Act who were exposed as adulterers within the next three years : 4

Chance that a woman first elected to the U.S. House or Senate before 1993 was a congressional widow : 1 in 4

Ratio of the 1998 divorce rate in New York State to the rate in Arkansas : 2:3

Chance that a U.S. man believes that oral sex does not constitute adultery : 1 in 8

Chance that a U.S. woman believes this : 1 in 9

Portion of all divorces that occur after more than four years of marriage : ⅔

Rank of people on their third marriage among spouses who say "I love you" most often : 1

Number of years the editor of *Divorce Magazine* spent working at *Wedding Bells* magazine : 3

Total number of marriages experienced by the two co-authors of *Staying Married and Loving It* : 5

Number of months one of them spent married to the original Bozo the Clown : 18

Modern Baby Making

Age, in years, of the first baby born in Denmark in January 2000, according to the hospital's computer : 100

Age in days of the McCaughey septuplets by the time they got their first agent : 20

Average number of I.Q. points by which the intelligence of an eight-year-old who was breast-fed exceeds that of one who was not : 8

Percentage change since 1984 in the average price paid in the U.S. for a month's worth of human eggs : +1,900

Price paid for six vials of frozen sperm in 1995 at a benefit auction for a Boston lesbian and gay health center : $825

Estimated number of frozen embryos disposed of by British fertility clinics in August 1996 : 5,500

Number whose disposal was requested by the couples that produced them : 2,500

Average number of months in prison to which two New Jersey teenagers were sentenced in 1998 for killing their newborn in a Delaware hotel room : 27

Estimated number of U.S. women arrested for child abuse between 1977 and 1998 for ingesting drugs or alcohol while pregnant : 200

Years in prison to which a South Carolina woman was sentenced for this in 1992 : 8

Percentage of welfare mothers in 1995 who were under the age of eighteen : 1.2

Percentage in 1999 : 0.93

Number of the four states with the highest illegitimacy rate in 1997 that were also among those in which the largest percentage of the population was on welfare : 2

Rank of Vermont and Mississippi among the states with the most generous welfare programs : 1,50

Rank of Vermont and Mississippi among the states with the highest birthrate among adolescents : 45,1

Percentage of Planned Parenthood donors in 1994 who also donated to the anti-abortion group Operation Rescue that year : 17

Factor by which the pregnancy-related death rate among African-American women exceeds that of white American women : 3.7

Percentage change since 1970 in the number of U.S. children born to one white and one non-white parent : +345

Rank of José, among the most popular names given boys born in California or Texas in 1998 : 1

Ranking points by which the name Monica dropped in popularity among those naming U.S. girls between 1997 and 1999 : 24

Family Affairs

Chance that a U.S. household consists of a husband, a wife, and their offspring : 1 in 4

Percentage of U.S. men between twenty-five and thirty-four who earn enough to keep a family of four from poverty : 71

Chance that a mother of dependent children depicted on a prime-time network TV show in 1998 held a paying job : 1 in 3

Chances that a nonfictional American mother with children did : 2 in 3

Percentage of female prison inmates who are mothers : 78

Number of states that enacted new abortion restrictions in 1996 : 9

Number that did in 1998 : 27

Ratio of the number of mothers who killed a son in 1997 to those who killed a daughter : 7:8

Ratio of the number of fathers who killed a son to those who killed a daughter : 7:8

Ratio of domestic murders in 1976 in which men were killed to those in which women were killed : 1:1

Ratio today : 2:5

Average number of U.S. public-school children per PTA member : 7

Number of U.S. parents who say they are as attached to their dogs as they are to their children : 6,200,000

Number of pups that Bob Dole's dog Leader has sired with Strom Thurmond's dog Chelsea Marie : 8

Percentage of Americans who said in 1998 that they would not want their twenty-one-year-old daughter to intern in the Clinton White House : 44

Number of years after 1993's Baby Jessica custody ruling that both her birth parents and her adoptive parents filed for divorce : 6

Weeks after giving birth to Michael Jackson's first child in 1997 that his wife returned to work as his plastic surgeon's assistant : 6

Number of his own children Ted Turner laid off during the merger of his company with Time Warner : 1

Chance that U.S. parents require that children do their homework before watching TV : 1 in 12

Factor by which having an overweight parent increases a child's chance of becoming obese : 2

Around the House

Average number of stars visible on a clear night from a U.S. suburb : 250

Average number visible from the wilderness : 2,500

Number of shades of white offered in Ralph Lauren's 1996 paint collection : 35

Price of a portable dungeon from Master R's, a Toronto company : $1,750

Days in jail served by a Michigan man in 1994 after being convicted of secretly videotaping people using his bathroom : 75

Ratio of Americans who said in 1996 that they "could not live without a blow-dryer" to those who felt that way about personal computers : 1:1

Number of high-resolution computer screens originally installed in the "video wall" of Bill Gates's house : 24

Chance that an American falls asleep with the TV on at least three nights a week : 1 in 4

Number of TV sets owned by Martha Stewart : 16

Number of phone lines connected to her five car phones : 7

Minimum number of steam cleanings that Stewart believes a car's engine should undergo each year : 1

Ratio of the air pollution generated by driving a car one hundred miles to the pollution generated by operating a leaf blower for one hour : 1:1

Percentage change between 1993 and 1995 in U.S. sales of manual push mowers : +150

Price of a mahogany-handled sterling-silver trowel, from Tiffany & Co. : $295

Estimated number of U.S. women who purchased their first chain saw in 1995 : 500,000

Estimated property damage caused in a New York suburb that year by a man firing a slingshot from his Lincoln : $7,000

Average number of days after U.S. clocks are set forward each spring that the fatal-accident rate declines to normal : 4

Hours of helicopter lessons required for the new "Super Butler" degree at London's most expensive butler school : 60

Number of kitchens in the home Mike Tyson put up for sale in 1997 : 7

Pounds of meat consumed daily by the household of the tenth-century emir of Cordova : 13,000

Number of women in his harem : 6,300

Days of peace the emir claimed to have known in his lifetime : 14

Edibles and Potables

Number of "food contacts" Americans have per day : 27

Number of states in which it is illegal to publicly disparage a particular foodstuff : 13

Number of state and county fairs that participated in the 1998 National Best Spam Recipe Contest : 77

Percentage by which the Pillsbury Bake-Off increased its grand prize in 1995 : 1,900

Number of months later that a man finally won it : 9

Percentage of Americans who describe "barbecue" as the aroma that best defines America : 39

First edition of *Joy of Cooking* not to include a recipe for a soup made from endangered turtles : 1997

Percentage change since 1988 in the portion of seafood eaten worldwide that is cultivated rather than caught : +146

Average pounds of wild ocean fish that a fish farm needs in order to produce a single pound of a carnivorous fish such as salmon : 5

Estimated portion of whale, dolphin, and porpoise meat consumed in Japan last year whose pollution levels were toxic : ½

Number of Britons seeking medical care in 1997 for injuries sustained while attempting to open cans of corned beef : 4,824

Ratio of annual per capita alcohol consumption in Russia to that in the U.S. : 3:8

Ratio of the average price of a gallon of milk to the average price of a gallon of gas in 1998 : 2:1

In 1999 : 2.5:1

Factor by which the sweetness of Sucralose, an artificial sweetener, exceeds that of sugar : 600

Percentage of first-year medical students who believe that a knowledge of nutrition is important to their career : 74

Percentage of third-year medical students who believe this : 13

Number of people who ingested E. coli bacteria as part of a Stanford Medical Center study between 1995 and 1998 : 65

Amount each participant was paid per day : $75

Number of people who developed food poisoning after attending a Connecticut Food Association reception in 1994 : 57

Estimated number of people who could be fed for one year with the food Americans waste in one day : 240,183

Suggested retail price of a packet of Diet Dirt, sterilized soil to be sprinkled over food to make it repugnant : $9.95

Rank of iron supplements among the most common cause of fatal poisoning for U.S. children under the age of six in 1992 : 1

Shelter

Ratio of the size of an average residence in Tokyo to the size of an average American two-car garage : 4:3

Percentage change between 1975 and 1998 in the size of a new U.S. home : +33

Percentage change between 1965 and 1995 in the number of U.S. households that pay for housecleaning : +53

Price of a two-day course in igloo building at the University of Calgary : $44

Hours required to assemble a prefabricated nuclear-bomb shelter, according to a 1961 *Life* magazine cover story : 4

Average number of structures that catch fire in the U.S. each hour : 60

Gallons of gasoline required to truck the shack in which Ted Kaczynski wrote his Unabomber manifesto from Montana to California in 1997 : 250

Number of people evacuated or detained from entering California buildings in December 1998 because of anthrax threats : 3,000

Factor by which the number of California foreclosures in 1998 exceeded those in 1990 : 4

Average number of months that an applicant waits to be placed in public housing, nationwide : 11

Average number of months an applicant waits in New York City : 96

Maximum income that an Aspen, Colorado, resident may earn in order to be eligible for public housing : $106,000

Units of public housing the federal government plans to demolish by the year 2003 : 100,920

Units it plans to construct by then : 24,679

Percentage change in the number of rural Americans living in mobile homes between 1980 and 1990 : +52

Number of conservation and anti-sprawl initiatives on state and local ballots in 1998 : 240

Percentage passed by voters : 72

Average number of rural acres lost to "urban sprawl" in the U.S. each year since 1970 : 1,000,000

VACATION

Holidays

Travel and Tourism

The Sporting Life

The Great Outdoors

Leisure Time

Junk Food

Sex

Holidays

Chances that a signature appended to the Declaration of Independence was put there on July 4, 1776 : 2 in 7

Ratio of eggs rolled on the White House lawn on Easter in 1999 to the number of bombs dropped on Serbia during its Orthodox holy week that year : 1:1

Estimated attendance at a "drive-through theater" reenactment of the crucifixion held each April in Maryland : 3,000

Number of U.S. cities that have declared March 13 "L. Ron Hubbard Day" : 291

Year in which Christmas celebrations, plum pudding, and mince pie were outlawed in England : 1647

Estimated number of U.S. children hospitalized in 1997 for injuries involving the ingestion of Christmas ornaments : 569

Number of confirmed U.S. deaths caused by doctored Halloween candy given to children by strangers : 0

Number of confirmed deaths caused by doctored Halloween candy given to children by their relatives : 1

Percentage of turkeys tested by the Department of Agriculture in 1996 and 1997 that were infected by campylobacteria : 90

Rank of campylobacteria among the most common bacterial causes of diarrheal illness in the U.S. : 1

Age, in years, of the oldest frozen turkey about which Butterball's hotline has ever fielded a "freshness" question : 23

Percentage of Americans who say they'd rather clean the basement, work on their taxes, or visit the dentist over their Thanksgiving holiday than go Christmas shopping : 62

Portion of the four pounds of butter the average American eats annually that is consumed after November 1 : ¼

Rank of milk among professional Santas' favorite drinks with cookies, according to the American Dairy Association : 1

Chance that a U.S. adult can name all of Santa's reindeer : 1 in 4

Chance that a character depicted in a Macy's Thanksgiving Day Parade balloon in 1997 was trademarked : 1 in 2

Average life span, in years, of a Macy's Thanksgiving Day Parade balloon : 25

Number of fireworks launched per second in New York City's July 4th display in 1977 : 4

Number launched per second in 1997's : 8

Year in which New York's Marriott Marquis hotel began taking reservations for New Year's Eve 1999 : 1983

Year in which the hotel opened : 1985

Travel and Tourism

Fuel mileage of the *QEII*, in feet per gallon : 29

Maximum daily number of tourists allowed at the Beatrix Potter cottage in Sawrey, England : 800

Number of business cards on exhibit at the Business Card Museum in Erdenheim, Pennsylvania : 50,000

Estimated change in attendance at America's top fifty theme parks between 1997 and 1998 : −2,000,000

Attendance at the first World Dracula Congress held in May 1995 in Bucharest : 200

Attendance two years later at "Dracula 97: A Centennial Celebration," held in Los Angeles : 600

Percentage of Americans who said in 1998 that they would rather vacation with O. J. Simpson than with Jack Kevorkian : 16

Price of "NowAge 2000," a seven-day cruise offering spiritual healing and contact with lost loved ones : $1,260

Average price of a cabin on *The Nation* magazine's first annual "*Nation* Cruise" to the Caribbean in 1998 : $2,800

Estimated average hourly wage of each of the cruise ship's Indonesian crew members : $2.47

Number of tourists taken hostage by striking Club Med workers in Martinique for three days in 1998 : 287

Percentage change since 1992 in the annual number of U.S. tourists visiting India : +61

Percentage change since 1987 in the number of Americans who go camping in R.V.s : −29

Number of espresso makers Sandy Hill Pittman took with her in 1996 on her third attempt to climb Mount Everest : 1

Average annual number of silver teaspoons reported missing from the Washington Hilton since 1996 : 13,500

Number of tourists who required emergency medical services in 1994 while waiting to tour the White House : 41

Number of times in the fall of 1998 that patrons unzipped the fly of the Bill Clinton wax figure at Madame Tussaud's in Sydney before the museum sewed it up : 120

Amount spent to construct an 80-foot replica of Mount Rushmore at Japan's Western Village theme park : $30,000,000

Amount spent in 1998 by Mount Vernon's directors to give George Washington's reputation more "sizzle" : $3,000,000

Price an Indiana historical museum charges visitors to spend ninety minutes as a runaway slave : $15

Price per person of having dinner in a turn-of-the-century kitchen in New York City's Lower East Side Tenement Museum : $200

Price of a day at Obertraun Schilcherhaus, an Austrian nudist cross-country skiing resort : $30

Ratio of the number of hotel rooms in Venice to the number planned for Las Vegas's Venetian Hotel : 1:1

Number of rooms planned for the Lunar Hilton : 5,000

The Sporting Life

Estimated number of days each year during which no major-league sports event takes place in the U.S. : 5

Percentage change since 1980 in the number of Americans who belong to a bowling league : −53

Percentage change since 1987 in the number of U.S. hunters : −29

Price of an "authentic" charcoal-lined U.S. military body bag from the *Sportsman's Guide* catalogue : $12.88

Price of a Waterford crystal vase inscribed with a picture of Larry Bird from the NBA's Manhattan boutique : $8,000

Factor by which male readership of *Sports Illustrated* increases for the swimsuit issue : 2

Factor by which female readership does : 4

Points by which the national Nielsen rating of the 1999 Women's World Cup exceeded that of the NBA finals : 2

Average percentage points by which a male sports fan's testosterone level rises when his team wins : 20

Average points by which it falls when they lose : 20

Number of Texas junior-high and high-school basketball coaches ejected from games in 1997 for "unsporting behavior" : 82

Minutes of tobacco chewing and spitting aired on the World Series broadcast in 1996 : 2.3

Minutes aired on the 1986 World Series broadcast : 23.9

Chance that an NBA player suffers from toenail fungus : 1 in 3

Total fines levied by the NBA during the 1997–98 season on players whose shorts were too long : $67,500

Rank of black among jersey colors worn in regular-season NHL games from 1991 through 1995 by teams receiving the most penalty minutes : 1

Estimated number of colleges that Newt Gingrich's high-school football coach queried in vain for a helmet big enough to fit his head : 5

Average number of dimples on a golf ball : 415

Amount Americans spent on golf clubs in 1998 : $2,430,000,000

Ratio of federal spending on Atlanta's homeless in preparation for the 1996 Summer Olympics to the city's average annual spending on the homeless in the preceding five years : 6:1

Number of months before the 1996 games that the planners began manufacturing ice for the event : 3.5

Estimated number of security staffers per athlete at the 1996 Olympics : 5

Number of Elvis impersonators hired to entertain in Atlanta's Olympic village : 3

Amount *Fortune* magazine estimates that Michael Jordan's NBA career has contributed to the U.S. economy : $10,000,000,000

Price of Spike Lee's two courtside seats at New York Knicks home games during the regular season in 1999 : $116,100

Average number of buffalo-meat hot dogs sold each football season at Denver's Mile High Stadium : 4,500

Percentage change since 1992 in the number of Americans who play touch football "frequently" : −4

Percentage change since 1988 in the number of Americans who snowboard : +228

Percentage change between 1987 and 1994 in the number of Americans who skateboard : –45

Percentage change since then : +37

Average amount spent on the tires used by each car during the Indianapolis 500 : $12,800

Length of the course used each August at New Jersey's Annual Cockroach Derby, in feet : 5.5

Price of renting a duck to compete in the annual Great American Duck Race held in Deming, New Mexico, each summer : $10

Number of trout and perch dumped into Russia's Lake Ukshe in July 1997 in preparation for a fishing trip by Boris Yeltsin : 10,000

Minutes of pregame snowball making allowed in Finland's annual International Snow Battle Contest held each April : 30

Number of Danes injured by falling soccer goalposts between 1989 and 1997 : 117

Rank of badminton among sports causing the largest number of eye injuries : 1

Number of years Charlie Brown flew kites before having his first bad experience with a tree : 4

The Great Outdoors

Acres of U.S. turf coated with lawn paint each year : 3,400

Chance that the annual median flow of an unfettered U.S. stream is greater than it was 50 years ago : 1 in 3

Average number of bacteria living in a pound of U.S. mud : 455,000,000,000

Ratio of bacteria living in a pound of mud to those living in a pound of dirt : 1,000:1

Percentage of Ford Explorer owners who have never taken their vehicles off-road : 87

Number of cars broken into by bears at Yosemite National Park in 1997 : 889

Percentage of U.S. National Park Service land that is in Alaska : 65

Ratio of miles of logging and other roads in U.S. national forests to the total length of the interstate highway system : 8:1

Ratio of the number of miles of highway in Minnesota to the number of miles of groomed snowmobile trails there : 2:3

Rank of cigarette butts among the most common debris found on U.S. shores during 1997's International Coastal Cleanup : 1

Number of artificial reefs planned for construction worldwide in 1998 to facilitate surfing : 4

Number of bathing suits sold in the U.S. per second : 4

Maximum portion of buttocks that one may legally bare in public in Manatee County, Florida : ⅔

Average number of hours per week that Bob Dole spent tanning in 1996 : 3.5

Amount of sunscreen he used : 0

Chances that a sunscreen labeled SPF 30 delivers an SPF below this : 4 in 5

Percentage by which the incidence of skin cancer rises for every 1 percent decrease in the size of the ozone layer : 2

Estimated percentage of worldwide ozone depletion since 1986 attributable to chemical products made by DuPont : 13

Percentage of U.S. plant species cited as "threatened by extinction" by the World Conservation Union in 1998 : 29

Number of flowers that prison inmates plant each spring at the Illinois State Fairgrounds : 110,000

Estimated number of concurrent "killer bee" stings that a healthy adult human can survive : 1,300

Estimated number of mosquito bites required to drain all the blood from a U.S. adult : 1,120,000

Estimated number of bug zappers required to kill all the insects in the world : 1,104,120,000,000

Leisure Time

Average duration in hours of the stupor induced in Japanese beetles by the consumption of geraniums : 8

Miles of doodles produced by the average sixth grader during the school year : 1.3

Date and time of the annual pi celebration held at San Francisco's Exploratorium : 3/14, 1:59

Average number of pies brought to each year's event since it began in 1988 : 30

Rank of Taurus among the most common astrological signs of Internet users : 1

Percentage of U.S. men who own a pair of Dockers khakis : 73

Pairs of jeans that Frank Sinatra owned in his lifetime : 0

Percentage of the 125 people included in 1999's *Flemings Who's Who in Central Banking* who list no "leisure pursuits" : 90

Percentage change since 1987 in the number of Americans who work out on a treadmill : +722

Average number of contestants in the Championship Race for Riding Lawn Mowers held each year on Labor Day weekend : 50

Length in minutes of Newt Gingrich's monthly head massage at the Bubbles hair salon in Washington, D.C. : 5

Estimated number of cigars George Burns smoked in his lifetime : 521,220

Percentage of Americans who believed in 1997 that they themselves were more likely to cheat at cards than Bill Clinton or Al Gore : 8

Number of people besides Al Gore who called the *Washington Post* in March 1998 to point out that a photo of the Earth had been published upside down : 0

Number of "Snapple enthusiasts" who attended a "Snapple Convention" held in a New York suburb in 1995 : 3,800

Hours that Shaquille O'Neal spent snowed in at a Pennsylvania hotel in January 1996 with the cast of "Sesame Street on Ice" : 45

Junk Food

Damages paid by the Kellogg Company in 1995 after an Ohio man claimed a flaming Pop-Tart ignited his kitchen : $2,400

Damages awarded Pizza Hut in 2000 after it sued a competitor whose ads claimed it made "better" pizza : $467,620

Number of Fowl Balls, a snack made from deep-fried turkey testicles, sold at Denver's Coors Field in 1996 : 243

Cans of beer the U.S. Navy requisitions for each sailor completing forty-five consecutive days at sea : 2

Fine introduced by Bermuda in 1997 for opening a McDonald's there : $5,000

Percentage of the thirty-five McDonald's in Washington, D.C., that the city has equipped with community policing stations : 35

Number of the world's ten busiest McDonald's franchises that are in Russia or Hong Kong : 3

Portion of McDonald's 1995 revenue that came from overseas : ½

Tons of sulfuric acid used each year at Kraft's gelatin plant in Woburn, Massachusetts : 2,035

Rank of Des Moines in per capita Jell-O consumption : 1

Pounds of chocolate consumed by the average American in a single year : 12

Quarts of Starbucks Java Chip ice cream found in the freezer of the Heaven's Gate compound in California after the group's mass suicide in 1997 : 7

Gallons of onion ice cream sold last summer at Vidalia restaurant in Washington, D.C. : 48

Estimated number of complimentary doughnuts Bob Dole received while under contract with Dunkin' Donuts : 2,880

Number he distributed to reporters waiting outside Monica Lewinsky's Watergate apartment on February 2, 1998 : 48

Number of Bill Clinton Waffles sold by a California bakery in the fall of 1996 : 50,000

Weight, in pounds, of a "Big Boy" statue stolen from a Toledo outlet of the Big Boy chain in March 1995 : 300

Number of days later that its parts were found strewn across the city accompanied by notes reading "Big Boy is dead!" : 2

Sex

Time at which Americans are most likely to have sex : 10:34 P.M.

Percentage of U.S. women who believe "a good night's sleep is better than sex" : 46

Average number of minutes an American spends making love, including foreplay, per session : 33.24

Average number of additional minutes women say they would like each session to last : 12

Chance that an impotence drug up for approval by the FDA in 1998 listed yawning as a side effect : 1 in 3

Number of homemade sex videos in *Penthouse* magazine's "Amateur" series : 2

Amount that Bear, Stearns's chairman donated to a New York hospital in June of 1998 to sponsor Viagra for the poor : $1,000,000

Amount that the Pentagon estimated it would spend on Viagra in 1999 : $50,000,000

Median percentage increase in penile blood flow among men exposed to the scent of roses : 4

Median percentage increase among men exposed to the combined scents of doughnuts and cola : 13

Price of a 2.5-ounce bottle of Donut Cologne, from the Donut Cologne Partnership : $6.95

Months after Bill Clinton's first inauguration that heterosexual fellatio was legalized in Washington, D.C. : 4

Number of states in which the practice is still illegal : 14

Ratio of the number of "cigar" references in the Starr report to the number of "Whitewater" references : 9:1

Attendance at Oklahoma Congressman Tom Coburn's first annual safe-sex slide show in 1995 : 170

Attendance at 1999's slide show : 230

Estimated number of Americans who die each year from auto-erotic asphyxiation : 750

Number of breasts from which Congressman Bob Barr licked whipped cream at a 1992 fund-raiser, according to a Georgia newspaper : 2

Factor by which a circumcised heterosexual man is more likely to receive oral sex than an uncircumcised one : 1.33

Percentage of U.S. prostitutes who exhibit the symptoms of post-traumatic stress disorder : 68

Percentage change since 1997 in the number of lawsuits filed against manufacturers of latex : +2,100

Rank of the U.S. among industrial democracies with the highest rate of sexual infidelity : 1

Price a Beverly Hills boutique charged in 1999 for a four-ounce bottle of shampoo containing a chemical found in human sperm : $25

Seating capacity of the Ménage à Trois Chair, available in 1996 from Kinky Joe's Erotic Furniture of New York City : 5

Year in which a medical dictionary defined heterosexuality as an "abnormal or perverted appetite" for the opposite sex : 1901

Chance that a U.S. woman over the age of forty made love in her clothes in the 1940s : 1 in 3

Chance that a woman under the age of forty did : 1 in 12

Number of pages accumulated in the FBI's "sex deviates" file by the time the program was abandoned in 1977 : 330,000

Number of years after Pee Wee Herman was arrested for masturbating in a public theater that his children's show was syndicated : 7

Number of months after Marv Albert was arrested for biting a prostitute that NBC announced it would rehire him : 2

Estimated number of hours a male june bug will cling to its partner after copulation : 2

RESOURCES

The sources below are arranged under the headings of the eighty-two categories listed in the table of contents. The numbering corresponds to the order of statistics under each rubric. In cases where the source for a statistic is a Web site, the Web address is provided; otherwise, the name of the individual or institution from which the statistic was derived is listed, followed by the source's geographical location. A slash indicates that we have combined information from more than one source; in cases where several such sources share one location, it is listed at the end of the entry. The citation "*Harper's* research" indicates that the magazine's staff has performed significant original research, reporting, and/or calculation. Most of the statistics in this volume were originally published in *Harper's Magazine* between April 1995 and January 2000. All were updated between July 1999 and February 2000. All figures have been adjusted for inflation where appropriate.

CIVICS

SCHOOL DAYS
1. ComedySportz (Los Angeles)
2. American Viewpoint, Inc. (Alexandria, Va.)
3. Dartmouth-Hitchcock Medical Center (Lebanon, N.H.)
4. Public Agenda (N.Y.C.)
5, 6. The Gallup Organization (Princeton, N.J.)
7. U.S. Department of Education/U.S. Department of Justice (Washington, D.C.)
8. U.S. Department of Agriculture (Washington, D.C.)

9. Taco Bell Corporation (Irvine, Calif.)
10. Student Achievements Services, Cherry Creek School District (Greenwood, Colo.)
11. U.S. District Court (Dayton, Ohio)
12. U.S. Department of Education (Washington, D.C.)
13. National School Safety Center (Westlake Village, Calif.)
14. National Center for Education Statistics (Washington, D.C.)
15. *Harper's* research
16. Chicago Board of Education/Chicago Public Schools
17. National Criminal Justice Reference Service (Rockville, Md.)/National School Safety Center (Westlake Village, Calif.)
18–21. National School Safety Center (Westlake Village, Calif.)
22. Superintendent, Lower Camden County Regional High School District 1 (Atco, N.J.)
23. General Accounting Office (Washington, D.C.)
24, 25. New York City Board of Education
26. Massachusetts Department of Education (Malden)
27. Psychemedics Corporation (Cambridge, Mass.)
28. National Commission on Teaching (N.Y.C.)
29, 30. Public Agenda Foundation (N.Y.C.)
31. The National PTA (Chicago)
32. Kansas State Department of Education (Topeka)

HIGHER EDUCATION

1. Center for Creative Leadership (Greensboro, N.C.)
2. National Education Data Resource Center (Alexandria, Va.)
3, 4. Peter Seldin, Pace University (N.Y.C.)
5. Phi Beta Kappa (Washington, D.C.)
6. *Harper's* research
7, 8. Jericho Communications (N.Y.C.)
9. U.S. Department of Education (Washington, D.C.)
10, 11. *Journal of Blacks in Higher Education* (N.Y.C.)
12, 13. Princeton University (Princeton, N.J.)
14. National Science Foundation (Arlington, Va.)/Cornell University (Ithaca, N.Y.)
15. Harvard Law School (Cambridge, Mass.)
16. Civil Rights Project, Harvard University (Cambridge, Mass.)
17, 18. Andrew Hacker, Queens College (N.Y.C.)
19. Office of Undergraduate Admissions at Harvard and Radcliffe (Cambridge, Mass.)
20, 21. American Council on Education (Washington, D.C.)
22. Harvard University (Cambridge, Mass.)

23. Borough of Manhattan Community College (N.Y.C.)
24. City University of New York (N.Y.C.)
25. Higher Education Research Institute, UCLA (Los Angeles)
26. National Science Foundation (Arlington, Va.)
27. *Multinational Monitor* (Washington, D.C.)
28. Smithsonian Associates Program (Washington, D.C.)

VOTERS AND VOTING

1. California Secretary of State Elections Division (Sacramento)
2. William C. Velásquez Institute (San Antonio, Tex.)
3, 4. Texas Secretary of State (Austin)
5, 6. A.F.L.-C.I.O. (Washington, D.C.)
7. U.S. Census Bureau (Washington, D.C.)
8. The Sentencing Project (Washington, D.C.)
9. Voter News Service (N.Y.C.)
10. Yankelovich Partners (Claremont, Calif.)
11–13. The Gallup Organization (Princeton, N.J.)
14. International Foundation for Election Systems (Washington, D.C.)
15. Nielsen Media Research (N.Y.C.)/Committee for the Study of the American Electorate (Washington, D.C.)
16. Oklahoma Democratic Party (Oklahoma City)
17. The Pew Research Center for the People and the Press (Washington, D.C.)
18. Libertarian Party (Washington, D.C.)
19, 20. *The Hotline* (Washington, D.C.)/Western Wats Opinion Research Center (Provo, Utah)

THE CAMPAIGN TRAIL

1. The Mellman Group (Washington, D.C.)
2. The House Administration Committee/The Senate Committee on Rules (Washington, D.C.)
3. The Center for Responsive Politics (Washington, D.C.)
4. Board of Elections (Chicago)
5. Republican National Committee (Washington, D.C.)
6. Campaign Study Group (Springfield, Va.)
7. Feren Communications (N.Y.C.)
8, 9. Gene Taft, *Going Negative*, Free Press (N.Y.C.)
10, 11. New Hampshire Department of Environmental Services (Concord, N.H.)
12, 13. Republican National Committee/Democratic National Committee (Washington, D.C.)

14–16. Sunshine Press Services, Inc. (Washington, D.C.)

17, 18. U.S. Senate Select Committee on Intelligence (Washington, D.C.)

19. Office of Senator Robert Torricelli (Washington, D.C.)

20, 21. Federal Election Commission (Washington, D.C.)

22, 23. *Harper's* research

24. *Fortune* (N.Y.C.)/The Center for Responsive Politics (Washington, D.C.)

25, 26. Feingold Senate Committee (Middleton, Wis.)/Federal Election Commission (Washington, D.C.)/Georgia Secretary of State (Atlanta)

27. Federal Election Commission (Washington, D.C.)

28. The Speaker's Press Office/The Speaker's Political Office (Washington, D.C.)

29. Fox News/Opinion Dynamics poll (N.Y.C.)

30. Common Cause (Washington, D.C.)

31–33. *Harper's* research

34, 35. Democratic National Committee/Republican National Committee (Washington, D.C.)/Carolyn Barta, *Dallas Morning News* (Dallas)

36. Federal Election Commission (Washington, D.C.)

37. Enfield Distribution (Enfield, N.H.)

38. *Harper's* research

39. Garrison Nelson, Brandeis University (Waltham, Mass.)

40, 41. Huckaby-Davis and Associates (Alexandria, Va.)

42. Office of the Governor (Austin, Tex.)

43. *Harper's* research

44. The New-York Historical Society (N.Y.C.)

45. Franklin D. Roosevelt Library (Hyde Park, N.Y.)

THE WHITE HOUSE

1. *Harper's* research

2. U.S. Senate Library (Washington, D.C.)

3, 4. White House Press Office (Washington, D.C.)

5. Legislative Resource Center (Washington, D.C.)

6, 7. White House/U.S. Office of Management and Budget (Washington, D.C.)

8. First Lady's Press Office (Washington, D.C.)

9. Office of Enforcement, U.S. Treasury Department (Washington, D.C.)

10, 11. Snack Food Association (Alexandria, Va.)/National Potato Promotion Board (Denver)

12. Office of Presidential Libraries (Washington, D.C.)/Chamber of Commerce (Hope, Ark.)
13. *New York Times*/CBS News poll (N.Y.C.)
14, 15. Fox News/Opinion Dynamics poll (N.Y.C.)
16. *Stanford Law Review* (Palo Alto, Calif.)/General Accounting Office (Washington, D.C.)
17. U.S. Department of Justice (Washington, D.C.)
18. Congressional Research Service (Washington, D.C.)/*Harper's* research
19. Department of Communication, University of Massachusetts (Amherst)
20. Republican National Committee (Washington, D.C.)
21. White House Curator's Office (Washington, D.C.)/*The New York Times* (N.Y.C.)
22. "President Clinton's Opposition to Motions of Paula Jones et al.," served in U.S. District Court, 11/13/97
23. Public Disclosure, Inc. (Washington, D.C.)
24. David Kendall, Williams & Connolly (Washington, D.C.)
25. White House Press Office (Washington, D.C.)
26. Office of the Independent Counsel (Washington, D.C.)/Mystic Seaport Museum (Mystic, Conn.)
27. *Who's Who in America*, Marquis Who's Who (New Providence, N.J.)
28. NBC News Poll (N.Y.C.)
29. The Roper Center (Storrs, Conn.)

THE CONGRESS

1. The Gallup Organization (Princeton, N.J.)
2. House Parliamentarian (Washington, D.C.)
3. Fox News/Opinion Dynamics poll (N.Y.C.)
4. Common Cause/Congressional Research Service (Washington, D.C.)
5, 6. Office of Senator Tom Daschle (Washington, D.C.)
7, 8. Senate Committee On Governmental Affairs (Washington, D.C.)
9. *The Hill*/*The Weekly Standard* (Washington, D.C.)
10. Girl Scouts of the U.S.A. (N.Y.C.)
11. Office of Senator Ron Wyden (Washington, D.C.)
12. Office of Senator Mitch McConnell (Washington, D.C.)/*Harper's* research
13. Howard M. Pearl (Chicago)
14, 15. Senate Committee on Banking, Housing, and Urban Affairs (Washington, D.C.)

16. Office of the Senate Sargeant at Arms/Office of Senator Daniel P. Moynihan (Washington, D.C.)
17. Congressional Subcommittee on International Relations and Human Rights (Washington, D.C.)
18, 19. Senate Committee on Foreign Relations (Washington, D.C.)
20. Citizens Against Government Waste (Washington, D.C.)
21. House Committee on Government Reform and Oversight (Washington, D.C.)
22. Federal Election Commission (Washington, D.C.)/*Harper's* research
23. *Roll Call* (Washington, D.C.)
24, 25. *Capitol Hill Blue* (Washington, D.C.)
26. Office of Senator Edward Kennedy/Congressional Accountability Project (Washington, D.C.)
27. *Roll Call* (Washington, D.C.)
28. Library of Congress (Washington, D.C.)/Gary Jacobson, University of California at San Diego
29. Architect of the Capitol (Washington, D.C.)

THE COURTS

1. Luntz Research Company (Arlington, Va.)
2. U.S. Department of Justice (Washington, D.C.)
3. *Harper's* research
4. American Bar Association (Chicago)
5, 6. U.S. Supreme Court (Washington, D.C.)
7. Administrative Office of the U.S. Courts (Washington, D.C.)
8. National Legal Aid and Defender Association (Washington, D.C.)
9. Don King Productions (Deerfield Beach, Fla.)
10, 11. Legal Services Corporation (Washington, D.C.)
12. State Senator Rodney Ellis (Austin, Tex.)
13. State Attorney's Office (Tallahassee, Fla.)
14, 15. Jones, Wyatt & Roberts (Enid, Okla.)
16. U.S. Attorney's Office (Oklahoma City)
17. Southern Center for Human Rights (Atlanta, Ga.)
18. Death Penalty Information Center (Washington, D.C.)
19, 20. Defender Association of Philadelphia
21. The City Attorney's Office, Criminal Division (Seattle)
22. California Legislative Analysts' Office (Sacramento)
23, 24. Legal Services Corporation (Washington, D.C.)
25, 26. Mitchell Banas (Buffalo, N.Y.)
27. Administrative Office of the U.S. Courts (Washington, D.C.)

28. Association of Trial Lawyers of America (Washington, D.C.)/National Center for State Courts (Williamsburg, Va.)
29. Technical Advisory Service for Attorneys (Blue Bell, Pa.)
30. *Harper's* research
31. Lewis Garrison (Memphis)

CRIME

1. CNN–*USA Today*–Gallup poll (Princeton, N.J.)
2. Mizell and Company International Security (Bethesda, Md.)
3, 4. Federal Bureau of Investigation (Washington, D.C.)
5. FBI Uniform Crime Reporting Program (Clarksburg, W.Va.)/Embassy of Canada (Washington, D.C.)/The Census Bureau Library (N.Y.C.)
6. Canadian Centre for Justice Statistics (Ottawa, Ontario)
7. Peter D. Hart Research Associates (Washington, D.C.)
8, 9. RAND (Santa Monica, Calif.)
10. Feminist Majority Foundation (Arlington, Va.)
11. The Alan Guttmacher Institute (N.Y.C.)
12, 13. The Linkup (Chicago)
14. U.S. Department of Justice (Washington, D.C.)
15. Fox News/Opinion Dynamics poll (N.Y.C.)
16. United States Attorney's Office (Los Angeles)
17. Osceola County Sheriff's Office (Osceola, Fla.)

PUNISHMENT

1. Bureau of Justice Statistics (Washington, D.C.)
2. Justice Policy Institute (Washington, D.C.)
3. Hugo Bedau, Tufts University (Medford, Mass.)
4, 5. California Department of Corrections (Sacramento)
6. Public Defender's Office (Orange County, Calif.)
7. Van Nuys Municipal Court (Van Nuys, Calif.)
8. California Department of Corrections (Sacramento)/U.S. Census Bureau (Washington, D.C.)
9. Los Angeles County Sheriff's Department
10. California Department of Corrections (Sacramento)
11. Delaware Department of Corrections (Smyrna)
12. Florida Department of Corrections (Tallahassee)
13. Limestone Correction Facility (Capshaw, Ala.)
14. Oklahoma Department of Corrections (Oklahoma City)
15. Rosen, Bien & Asaro (San Francisco)
16. Federal Bureau of Prisons (San Francisco)
17, 18. Bernalillo County Detention Center (Albuquerque, N. Mex.)

19. Maricopa County Sheriff's Office (Phoenix)
20. Central Intelligence Agency (Langley, Va.)
21. U.S. Attorney's Office (Washington, D.C.)
22. Chamber of Commerce (McAlester, Okla.)
23. Cumberland County Jail Records (Portland, Maine)

SOCIAL STUDIES

THE DRUG WAR

1. Centers for Disease Control and Prevention (Atlanta)/National Clearinghouse for Alcohol and Drug Information (Rockville, Md.)
2. Office of Representative Ed Whitfield (Washington, D.C.)
3. *Journal of Clinical Oncology* (Chestnut Hill, Mass.)
4, 5. Office of National Drug Control Policy (Washington, D.C.)
6, 7. UCLA Higher Education Research Institute (Los Angeles)
8. National Center for Juvenile Justice (Pittsburgh)/Substance Abuse and Mental Health Services Administration (Rockville, Md.)
9, 10. Office of National Drug Control Policy/Department of Health and Human Services (Washington, D.C.)
11. Federal Bureau of Investigation (Clarksburg, W. Va.)
12. U.S. Sentencing Commission (Washington, D.C.)
13, 14. The National Center on Addiction and Substance Abuse (N.Y.C.)
15, 16. Bureau of Justice Statistics Special Report, January 1999 (Washington, D.C.)
17. Wyoming Methamphetamine Initiative (Cheyenne)
18. Orange County District 9 Medical Examiner's Office (Orlando, Fla.)
19. U.S. Bureau for International Narcotics and Law Enforcement Affairs (Washington, D.C.)
20. Central Intelligence Agency (Langley, Va.)/U.N. Drug Control and Crime Prevention Committee (Geneva, Switzerland)
21, 22. Department of Defense (Arlington, Va.)
23. U.S. Customs (Washington, D.C.)
24. Mark Kleinman, UCLA (Los Angeles)
25. D.A.R.E. America (Los Angeles)
26. *Journal of Consulting and Clinical Psychology* (Philadelphia)
27. IMS America (Plymouth Meeting, Pa.)
28, 29. Daniel Safer, Johns Hopkins University School of Medicine (Baltimore)

30. Food and Drug Administration (Rockville, Md.)
31. Colleen Wolstenholme (Vancouver, British Columbia)
32. Executive Collectibles (Newport Beach, Calif.)
33. Partnership for a Drug-Free America (N.Y.C.)
34. David P. Phillips, University of California at San Diego
35. *New York Daily News* (N.Y.C.)

THE BATTLE OF THE SEXES

1, 2. James R. Petersen, *The Century of Sex,* Grove Press (N.Y.C.)
3, 4. *Harper's* research
   5. WNBA (N.Y.C.)
6, 7. U.S. Census Bureau (Washington, D.C.)
   8. International Mass Retail (Arlington, Va.)
   9. Pew Research Center for the People and the Press (Washington, D.C.)
  10. Office of the Senate Curator (Washington, D.C.)
11, 12. Bureau of Justice Statistics (Washington, D.C.)
  13. State Senator Dorothy Ruppert (Boulder, Colo.)
14, 15. Permanent Mission of Afghanistan to the United Nations (N.Y.C.)
  16. Pakistan Mission to the United Nations (N.Y.C.)
  17. Equal Employment Opportunity Commission (Washington, D.C.)/Mitsubishi (Normal, Ill.)
  18. The National Center for Public Policy Research (Washington, D.C.)
19, 20. Fox News/Opinion Dynamics poll (N.Y.C.)
  21. *The Weekly Standard* (Washington, D.C.)
  22. Dauphin County District Attorney's Office (Harrisburg, Pa.)
23, 24. Fox News/Opinion Dynamics poll (N.Y.C.)

BLACK AND WHITE

  1. 1996 National Black Election Study (Columbus, Ohio)
  2. Bureau of Labor Statistics (Washington, D.C.)
3, 4. U.S. Census Bureau (Washington, D.C.)
  5. National Criminal Justice Reference Service (Rockville, Md.)/U.S. Census Bureau (Washington, D.C.)
  6. *Harper's* research
7–10. U.S. Department of Justice (Washington, D.C.)
  11. NAACP Legal Defense and Educational Fund, Inc. (N.Y.C.)/National Coalition to Abolish the Death Penalty (Washington, D.C.)
  12. Federal Bureau of Prisons (Washington, D.C.)/South Dakota Department of Corrections (Pierre)/U.S. Census Bureau (Washington, D.C.)

13, 14. Flagstar Companies, Inc. (Spartanburg, S.C.)

15, 16. *Esquire* (N.Y.C.)

    17. William Lee Miller, *Arguing About Slavery*, Knopf (N.Y.C.)

    18. U.S. Census Bureau (Washington, D.C.)

19, 20. *Forbes* (N.Y.C.)

21, 22. Keeneland Library (Lexington, Ky.)

23, 24. Public Agenda (N.Y.C.)

25–27. William Lee Miller, *Arguing About Slavery*, Knopf (N.Y.C.)

    28. Juneteenth U.S.A. (Houston)

    29. Council of State Governments (Lexington, Ky.)

    30. Mississippi Senate Docket Room (Jackson)

    31. Tennessee State Legislature/Legislative Service Bureau (Nashville)

    32. Office of Senator Strom Thurmond (Washington, D.C.)

    33. Architect of the Capitol (Washington, D.C.)

    34. Clinton/Gore '96 (Washington, D.C.)

35, 36. Fox News/Opinion Dynamics poll (N.Y.C.)

    37. *Harvard Law Review* (Cambridge, Mass.)

38, 39. Boalt Hall, School of Law, University of California at Berkeley

    40. *Journal of Blacks in Higher Education* (N.Y.C.)

    41. CNDC Gallup poll (Princeton, N.J.)

CHILDHOOD

    1. U.S. Department of Health and Human Services/Social Security Administration/U.S. Department of Agriculture (Washington, D.C.)

    2. Annie E. Casey Foundation (Baltimore)

3, 4. Ellen Galinsky, *Ask the Children*, William Morrow and Co. (N.Y.C.)

    5. Frank Furstenberg, University of Pennsylvania (Philadelphia)

    6. National Center for Youth Law (San Francisco)

    7. U.S. Department of Health and Human Services (Washington, D.C.)

8, 9. Consumer Product Safety Commission (Bethesda, Md.)

    10. American Academy of Orthopaedic Surgeons (Rosemont, Ill.)

    11. National Cancer Institute (Bethesda, Md.)

    12. Eli Lilly & Co. (Indianapolis)

    13. Jericho Communications, Inc. (N.Y.C.)

14, 15. American Anti-Slavery Group (Somerville, Mass.)

    16. Girls Scouts of the U.S.A. (N.Y.C.)

    17. Edge Marketing (Charlotte, N.C.)

    18. Delta Dental Plan of Minnesota (Minneapolis)

19. *Zillions* magazine/Consumers Union (Yonkers, N.Y.)
20. Center for Media and Public Affairs (Washington, D.C.)
21. Leonard D. Eron et al., *Reason to Hope: A Psychological Perspective on Violence & Youth*, American Psychological Association (Washington, D.C.)
22, 23. Jim McNeal, Texas A&M University (Bryan, Tex.)
24. Campbell Mithun Esty (Minneapolis)

ADOLESCENCE

1. Public Agenda (N.Y.C.)
2. Children Now (Oakland, Calif.)
3. Fairbank, Maslin, Maulin & Associates (Los Angeles)
4. U.S. Conference of Mayors (Washington, D.C.)
5. Dean Victor Streib, Ohio Northern University (Ada, Ohio)
6, 7. National Center for Juvenile Justice (Pittsburgh)
8, 9. Family Research Laboratory, University of New Hampshire (Durham)
10, 11. Michael J. Axe, MD (Newark, Del.)
12, 13. New York State Department of Health (Albany)
14, 15. Institute for Social Research, University of Michigan (Ann Arbor)
16. University of Arizona (Tucson)
17. The Gallup Organization (Princeton, N.J.)
18. *Journal of the American Medical Association* (Chicago)

MODERN MATURITY

1. U.S. Census Bureau (Washington, D.C.)
2. American Association of Retired Persons (Washington, D.C.)
3. U.S. Senate Budget Committee (Washington, D.C.)
4. Kennedy Space Center (Cape Canaveral, Fla.)
5. *Harper's* research
6. Nation Institute (N.Y.C.)/Marttila & Kiley Inc. (Boston)
7. David Hinton (Nashville)
8, 9. American Jewish Committee (N.Y.C.)/Simon Wiesenthal Center (Los Angeles)
10. National Tax Payers' Union (Alexandria, Va.)
11. Criminal Justice Institute (Middletown, Conn.)
12. U.S. Department of Justice (Washington, D.C.)
13. General Accounting Office (Washington, D.C.)
14. http://www.leary.com
15. American Association of Retired Persons (Washington, D.C.)
16. Giovanni Gambassi, Brown University (Providence, R.I.)

17. Fox News/Opinion Dynamics poll (N.Y.C.)
18. *Wall Street Journal* (N.Y.C.)/NBC News poll (Washington, D.C.)
19. *Outlaw Biker* (Hoboken, N.J.)
20. Elizabeth Dole for President Exploratory Committee (Arlington, Va.)
21. National Sporting Goods Association (Mt. Prospect, Ill.)
22. U.S. Census Bureau (Washington, D.C.)

TRADITIONS

1. The Tea Council, Ltd. (London, England)
2. Gloustershire Echo (Gloustershire, England)
3. *Daily Star* (London, England)
4. Biosurgical Research Unit, Princess of Wales Hospital (South Wales, England)
5–7. *Harper's* research
8. Bil Keane (Laguna Beach, Calif.)
9. Enterprise (Bangkok, Thailand)
10. Nagoya City Representative's Office (Los Angeles)
11. Bryn Mawr College (Bryn Mawr, Pa.)
12. Sacred Well Congregation (San Antonio)
13. Army and Air Force Exchange (Dallas)/Navy Exchange Service Command (Virginia Beach, Va.)
14. Boy Scouts of America (Irving, Tex.)
15. Chatham-Effingham Liberty Regional Library (Savannah)
16. Alameda Cremations (Alameda, Calif.)
17, 18. American Institute of Physics (College Park, Md.)

GIVING AND RECEIVING

1. Gold Fields Mineral Service Ltd. (London, England)
2. Anatomical Chart Company (Skokie, Ill.)
3, 4. New England Confectionary Company (Cambridge, Mass.)
5. The Unity Center of Peace Church (Chapel Hill, N.C.)
6. Los Angeles Catholic Worker (Los Angeles)
7. Eric Hobsbawm, *The Age of Revolution*, Vintage (N.Y.C.)
8. State Department of Argentina (Buenos Aires)
9. *New England Journal of Medicine* (Boston)
10. Ann E. Kaplan, ed., *Giving USA*, American Association of Fund-Raising Counsel Trust for Philanthropy (Sewickley, Pa.)
11. Pallotta Teamworks of L.A. (Los Angeles)
12. First Lady's Press Office (Washington, D.C.)
13, 14. Office of Tipper Gore (Washington, D.C.)

15. Stanley Kutler, *Abuse of Power: The New Nixon Tapes*, The Free Press (N.Y.C.)
16, 17. Cast the Sleeping Elephant Trust (N.Y.C.)
18. *Hustler* (Los Angeles)
19, 20. Center on Budget and Policy Priorities (Washington, D.C.)
21. Hope Enterprises, Inc. (Burbank, Calif.)
22, 23. Studs Terkel (Chicago)

MAKING IT BIG

1. International Society of Cryptozoology (Tucson, Ariz.)
2. Marvel Comics (Los Angeles)
3. Department of Justice (Washington, D.C.)
4. Harry Walker Agency (N.Y.C.)
5, 6. Buchanan 2000, Inc. (McLean, Va.)
7. Kruse International (Auburn, Ind.)
8, 9. CBS Entertainment Communications (N.Y.C.)
10. National Conference of Catholic Bishops (Washington, D.C.)
11. United Network for Organ Sharing (Richmond, Va.)/Southwest Organ Bank (Dallas)
12. Mo' Better Meaty Meat Burger (Los Angeles)
13. Fox News/Opinion Dynamics poll (N.Y.C.)
14. Architect of the Capitol (Washington, D.C.)
15, 16. Human Rights Campaign (Washington, D.C.)/Gay and Lesbian Alliance Against Defamation (N.Y.C.)
17, 18. Mattel Inc. (El Segundo, Calif.)/Raytheon Company (Lexington, Mass.)/Zsa Zsa Gabor (Los Angeles)
19. Patricia Schroeder (Washington, D.C.)
20. Gerald Ford Presidential Library (Ann Arbor, Mich.)
21. Susan Jonas and Marilyn Nissenson, *Going, Going, Gone*, Chronicle Books (San Francisco)
22. *Playboy* (Chicago)
23. WNBC (N.Y.C.)
24. Robert M. Motta (Oak Park, Ill.)
25. http://www.uq.oz.au/~micoddy/gacy/catalogue.html
26. Gallery of History (Las Vegas)
27. Jones, Wyatt & Roberts (Enid, Okla.)
28. America's Talking (Fort Lee, N.J.)
29, 30. Buckingham Palace (London, England)
31. Christie's (N.Y.C.)
32. Tom Breslin, *An American Legend*, General Publishing Group (Santa Monica, Calif.)/New Jersey Department of Health and Senior Services (Trenton)

HISTORY

16. Caviar House (London, England)
17, 18. U.S. Department of State (Washington, D.C.)
19. Dennis Papazian, Center for the Study of Russia, University of Michigan (Dearborn)
20. Kansas State University (Manhattan, Kans.)
21, 22. Volkswagen (Wolfsburg, Germany)
23, 24. Department of Veterans' Affairs (Washington, D.C.)
25. California Employment Development Department (Sacramento)
26, 27. General Accounting Office (Washington, D.C.)
28. Senate Appropriations Committee (Washington, D.C.)
29, 30. The Gallup Organization (Princeton, N.J.)/Center for Defense Information/Center for Military History (Washington, D.C.)/*Harper's* research
31. *Truman*, The American Experience, WGBH (Boston)
32, 33. Tore Ulving Art Auctions (Toensberg, Norway)
34. Atlanta Project, The Carter Center (Atlanta)
35. U.S. Joint Staff (Washington, D.C.)/U.S. European Command (Stuttgart, Germany)/U.S. Central Command (Macdill A.F.B., Tampa, Fla.)
36. Fox News/Opinion Dynamics poll (N.Y.C.)
37. CBS News poll (N.Y.C.)

ARMS AND ARMAMENTS

1, 2. Congressional Research Service (Washington, D.C.)
3. Federation of American Scientists (Washington, D.C.)
4, 5. World Policy Institute (N.Y.C.)
6. General Accounting Office (Washington, D.C.)
7. Defense Logistics Agency (Fort Belvoir, Va.)
8. U.S. Air Force (Arlington, Va.)
9. Federal Bureau of Investigation/*U.S. News & World Report* (Washington, D.C.)
10. John France, *Western Warfare in the Age of the Crusades, 1000–1300*, Cornell University Press (Ithaca, N.Y.)
11. Center for Defense Information (Washington, D.C.)
12. China North Industries Corp. (Beijing)/Human Rights Watch (Washington, D.C.)
13. Jack Couffer, *Bat Bomb*, University of Texas Press (Austin)
14, 15. The Gallup Organization (Princeton, N.J.)
16, 17. Economic Policy Institute (Washington, D.C.)
18, 19. Center for Defense Information (Washington, D.C.)
20. Office of Senator Trent Lott (Washington, D.C.)
21. U.S. Navy (Arlington, Va.)

22. Center for Defense Information (Washington, D.C.)
23. U.S. House Defense Appropriations Committee (Washington, D.C.)
24, 25. Ballistic Missiles Defense Organization (Arlington, Va.)
26, 27. Natural Resources Defense Council (Washington, D.C.)
28. Center for Defense Information (Washington, D.C.)
29. The Brookings Institution (Washington, D.C.)
30. Coalition to Reduce Nuclear Dangers (Washington, D.C.)
31. *Harper's* research

MILITARY PERSONNEL

1, 2. Center for Defense Information (Washington, D.C.)
3. Department of Veterans' Affairs (Washington, D.C.)
4, 5. Embassy of the Republic of Korea (Washington, D.C.)
6. U.S. Department of Defense (Arlington, Va.)
7. Center for Military History (Washington, D.C.)/United Nations (N.Y.C.)
8. Embassy of Russia (Washington, D.C.)/Doctors Without Borders (N.Y.C.)
9. Deutsche Bank (Frankfurt, Germany)
10. *Harper's* research
11. U.S. Veterans' Administration (Washington, D.C.)
12. Canadian National Defense Department (Ottawa, Ontario)
13, 14. U.S. Department of Defense (Washington, D.C.)
15. General Accounting Office (Washington, D.C.)
16. U.S. Department of Defense (Arlington, Va.)
17. *Washington Times* (Washington, D.C.)
18. Department of the Air Force/Department of the Navy/Department of the Army/United States Marine Corps (Washington, D.C.)
19. Department of the Air Force (Washington, D.C.)
20. Office of the Under Secretary of Defense (Washington, D.C.)
21–23. U.S. Department of Defense (Arlington, Va.)
24, 25. U.S. Naval Academy (Annapolis, Md.)
26. Harvard Medical School (Belmont, Mass.)

THE COURSE OF EMPIRE

1, 2. Center for Defense Information (Washington, D.C.)
3, 4. World Policy Institute (N.Y.C.)
5. U.S. Department of Defense (Arlington, Va.)/Congressional Budget Office (Washington, D.C.)
6. Center for Defense Information (Washington, D.C.)
7. *Far Eastern Economic Review* (Hong Kong)

8, 9. The Hong Kong Transition Project (Hong Kong)
10. Shel Jacobs Law Firm/York University (Toronto, Ontario)
11. Library of Indian Affairs (Quebec)
12. U.S. Bureau of Indian Affairs (Washington, D.C.)
13, 14. Rick LaFleur, University of Georgia (Athens)
15. Brian Richardson, University of Leeds (England)
16. Eric Hobsbawm, *Nations and Nationalism Since 1780*, Cambridge University Press (N.Y.C.)
17, 18. Eric Hobsbawm, *The Age of Revolution: 1789–1848*, Random House (N.Y.C.)
19. The Gallop Organization (New Maiden, England)
20. Church of Jesus Christ of Latter-day Saints (Cambridgeshire, England)
21. Department of Information and Public Relations, Government of the British Virgin Islands (Tortola, British Virgin Islands)
22. Greenbrier High School (Evans, Ga.)
23. Philip Morris International (Rye Brook, N.Y.)
24. McDonald's Corp. (Oak Brook, Ill.)/World Priorities Inc. (Washington, D.C.)

DIPLOMACY

1. Center for Defense Information (Washington, D.C.)
2. UNESCO (Paris)
3. Congressional Research Service (Washington, D.C.)
4. U.S. Department of State (Washington, D.C.)
5. U.S. Department of Defense (Arlington, Va.)
6. U.S. Department of State (Washington, D.C.)
7. Amnesty International (N.Y.C)/U.S. Department of Defense (Arlington, Va.)
8. United Nations (N.Y.C.)
9. Embassy of Turkey (Washington, D.C.)
10. *Harper's* research
11. Hard Rock Cafe, International (Orlando, Fla.)/U.S. Department of State (Washington, D.C.)
12. Foreign Agents Registration Unit, U.S. Department of Justice (Washington, D.C.)
13. Hyundai Motor America (Fountain Valley, Calif.)
14. Royal Dutch Shell Group (London, England)
15. Secretary of Culture of Argentina (Buenos Aires)
16. Office of the White House Press Secretary (Washington, D.C.)
17. *Soldier of Fortune* (Boulder, Colo.)/National Security Council (Washington, D.C.)

18, 19. Microsoft (Moscow, Russia)/Waggener Edstrom (Portland, Oreg.)
20. ARAMARK (Philadelphia)
21. *The Charlie Rose Show* (N.Y.C.)

SECRETS

1. Central Intelligence Agency (Langley, Va.)
2. Nick Cullather, Indiana University (Bloomington)
3, 4. Tim Weiner, *Blank Check: The Pentagon's Black Budget*, Warner Books (N.Y.C.)/Center for National Security Studies (Washington, D.C.)/Central Intelligence Agency (Langley, Va.)
5. *Time* (Washington, D.C.)/ABC News (Moscow, Russia)
6, 7. James Ledbetter (N.Y.C.)
8. Natural Resources Defense Council (Washington, D.C.)
9. Electronic Frontier Foundation (San Francisco)
10. Central Intelligence Agency (Langley, Va.)
11. *Scottish Sun* (Glasgow, Scotland)
12, 13. National Archives and Records Administration (College Park, Md.)
14. U.S. Court of Appeals/General Accounting Office (Washington, D.C.)
15. House Committee on Government Reform and Oversight (Washington, D.C.)
16, 17. *Legal Times*/Federal Bureau of Investigation (Washington, D.C.)
18. Central Intelligence Agency (Langley, Va.)
19. Sylvia Jukes Morris (Washington, D.C.)
20. Noèl Riley Fitch (Los Angeles)
21. Office of George Bush (Kennebunkport, Maine)

DÉJÀ VU

1. Willis Fletcher Johnson, *The History of Cuba*, B. F. Buck & Company (N.Y.C.)
2. Republican National Committee (Washington, D.C.)
3. *Harper's* research
4. *Forbes* (N.Y.C.)
5, 6. California Department of Motor Vehicles (Sacramento)
7. *Los Angeles Times* poll (Los Angeles)
8. George W. Bush for President (Austin, Tex.)
9, 10. Phoebus Auction Gallery (Hampton, Va.)
11. U.S. Space & Rocket Center (Huntsville, Ala.)
12. Los Alamos Study Group (Santa Fe, N. Mex.)
13, 14. Office of Representative Lane Evans (Washington, D.C.)
15, 16. James P. Linn (Oklahoma City)

17. State Prison of Vridsloeselille (Denmark)
18. *Kearney Courier* (Kearney, Mo.)
19. Federal Emergency Management Agency (Raleigh, N.C.)
20. The American Society of Plastic and Reconstructive Surgeons (Arlington Heights, Ill.)

GEOGRAPHY

STATE OF THE WORLD

1, 2. Benjamin Forest, Dartmouth College (Hanover, N.H.)
   3. United Nations Research Institute (Geneva, Switzerland)
   4. Institute for Policy Studies (Washington, D.C.)
   5. U.S. International Trade Commission (Washington, D.C.)
   6. Business Alliance for International Economic Development (Washington, D.C.)
7, 8. *American Banker* (N.Y.C.)
9, 10. World Bank (Washington, D.C.)
11, 12. World Bank (Washington, D.C.)/*Globe and Mail* (Toronto, Ontario)
13, 14. Home Office Research, Development and Statistics Directorate (London, England)
   15. Jim Seymour, East Asian Institute, Columbia University (N.Y.C.)/Bureau of Justice Statistics (Washington, D.C.)
16–18. United Nations (N.Y.C.)
   19. U.S. Department of State (Washington, D.C.)
   20. United Nations (N.Y.C.)
   21. International Maritime Bureau (Essex, England)
   22. Jeffrey T. Richelson, *The U.S. Intelligence Community*, Westview Press (Boulder, Colo.)/United Nations (N.Y.C.)
23, 24. National Geographic Society (Washington, D.C.)
   25. Bureau of Labor Statistics (Washington, D.C.)/*Harper's* research
   26. Canadian Hockey Association/Canadian Healthcare Association (Ottawa, Ontario)
   27. National Basketball Association (N.Y.C.)
   28. James R. Flynn, University of Otago (Dunedin, New Zealand)

AFRICA

1. Fernand Braudel, *A History of Civilizations*, Penguin (N.Y.C.)
2. U.S. Department of State (Washington, D.C.)
3. Embassy of the United States (Monrovia, Liberia)
4. Embassy of Tunisia (Washington, D.C.)

5. National Security Council (Washington, D.C.)
6. National Defense Headquarters (Ottawa, Ontario)
7. Doctors Without Borders (N.Y.C.)
8. Neiman Marcus (Dallas)
9. Pan American Health Organization (Washington, D.C.)
10. ActUp (N.Y.C.)/Worldbank Association (Washington, D.C.)
11. ActUp (N.Y.C.)
12. U.S. Census Bureau (Washington, D.C.)
13. Transparency International (Berlin, Germany)
14. Ronald Inglehart, University of Michigan (Ann Arbor)
15. Harvard University (Cambridge, Mass.)/World Bank (Washington, D.C.)
16. UNICEF (N.Y.C.)
17. World Health Organization (Washington, D.C.)
18. Amnesty International (N.Y.C.)
19. United Nations (N.Y.C.)
20. Independent Complaints Directorate (Pretoria, South Africa)
21. Detainees' Parents Support Committee (Johannesburg, South Africa)
22. Natal Law Society (Pietermaritzburg, South Africa)
23, 24. Robben Island (South Africa)

ASIA

1. Mark Elvin, *The Pattern of the Chinese Past*, Stanford University Press (Stanford, Calif.)
2. The Brookings Institution (Washington, D.C.)
3, 4. The Gallup Organization (Princeton, N.J.)
5. Embassy of China (Washington, D.C.)
6. World Vision (Washington, D.C.)
7. Dan Murphy, MD, Motael Clinic (Dili, Indonesia)
8. David Chandler, Cornell University (Ithaca, N.Y.)
9. Ellen Cogen, Jewish Theological Seminary (N.Y.C.)
10. Jones Lang Wootton (Hong Kong)
11. *Roll Call* (Washington, D.C.)
12, 13. Senate Foreign Relations Committee (Washington, D.C.)
14. Hillary Rodham Clinton Fan Club (Atlanta)
15. Embassy of India (Washington, D.C.)
16. Arms Control Association (Washington, D.C.)
17–19. Felipe Fernández-Armesto, *Millennium: A History of the Last Thousand Years*, Touchstone (N.Y.C.)
20. Jared Diamond, *Guns, Germs, and Steel*, W. W. Norton & Company (N.Y.C.)

21. David S. Landes, *The Wealth and Poverty of Nations*, W. W. Norton (N.Y.C.)

22–24. Embassy of Japan (Washington, D.C.)

25. Embassy of the Vatican (Washington, D.C.)

26, 27. Embassy of Vietnam (Washington, D.C.)

28, 29. International Institute for Strategic Studies (London, England)

30. Ministry of the Environment (Singapore)

31. The Trade and Human Rights Project (Seattle)

32. *Time* (N.Y.C.)

33. Taipei Economic and Cultural Representative Office in the United States (N.Y.C.)

RUSSIA

1. Center for International Sociological Studies (Moscow, Russia)

2. Embassy of Russia (Washington, D.C.)

3. Russian Center for Public Opinion and Market Research (Moscow, Russia)

4. Embassy of Russia (Washington, D.C.)

5, 6. U.S. Department of State (Washington, D.C.)

7. Russian Research Center Library (Cambridge, Mass.)

8. Russian Center for Public Opinion and Market Research (Moscow, Russia)

9. World Health Organization (Copenhagen, Denmark)/*Harper's* research

10. Soldiers' Mothers Committee (St. Petersburg, Russia)

11. Ellen Barry, *Moscow Times* (Moscow, Russia)

12. Bloomberg (N.Y.C.)/Distilled Spirits Council of the U.S. (Washington, D.C.)

13. U.S. Department of Commerce (Washington, D.C.)

14. U.S. Department of State (Washington, D.C.)/New York City Office of Management and Budget

15. Jewish Agency for Israel (Moscow, Russia)

16. Pizza Hut (Dallas)

17. Central Intelligence Agency (Langley, Va.)

18. Brookings Institution (Washington, D.C.)

THE MIDDLE EAST

1. Planet Hollywood Inc. (Orlando, Fla.)

2. *Harper's* research

3. International Monetary Fund (Washington, D.C.)

4–6. Felipe Fernández-Armesto, *Millennium: A History of the Last Thousand Years*, Touchstone (N.Y.C.)/Richard Bulliet, Columbia University (N.Y.C.)

7. Foundation for Middle East Peace (Washington, D.C.)
8. Peace Now (Jerusalem)
9, 10. Jerusalem Institute for Israel Studies (Jerusalem)
11, 12. Jerome M. Segal, University of Maryland (College Park)
13. National Council of Resistance of Iran (Washington, D.C.)
14. U.S. Department of State (Washington, D.C.)
15. United Nations (N.Y.C.)
16. The Mission of the Republic of Iraq to the United Nations (N.Y.C.)/American Petroleum Institute (Washington, D.C.)
17–20. Energy Information Administration (Washington, D.C.)
21, 22. U.S. Department of State (Washington, D.C.)
23, 24. Senate Committee on Banking, Housing, and Urban Affairs (Washington, D.C.)
25. United Nations Security Council (N.Y.C.)
26. International Action Center (N.Y.C.)
27. Human Rights Arms Project (Washington, D.C.)
28. Consulate General of Israel (N.Y.C.)/Embassy of Lebanon (Washington, D.C.)
29. B'tselem (Jerusalem)
30. Jerusalem Media Communications Center (Jerusalem)
31. Consulate General of Israel (N.Y.C.)
32. Associated Press Television News Library (London, England)

EUROPE

1, 2. Eric Hobsbawm, *The Age of Revolution*, Vintage (N.Y.C.)
3. Hearing before the Senate Select Intelligence Committee, 12/4/96 (Washington, D.C.)
4. Hearing before the House Committee on Appropriations, 3/12/94 (Washington, D.C.)
5. Center for Defense Information (Washington, D.C.)
6. Northern Ireland Police Authority (Belfast, Ireland)
7. Consulate General of Ireland (N.Y.C.)/Northern Ireland Police Authority (Belfast, Ireland)
8, 9. Ronald Inglehart, University of Michigan (Ann Arbor)
10. Delegation of the Commission of the European Communities (N.Y.C.)
11, 12. Organization for Economic Cooperation and Development (Washington, D.C.)
13. Taxpayer Association of Germany (Düsseldorf)
14, 15. Embassy of France (Washington, D.C.)
16. Royal Norwegian Consulate General (N.Y.C.)
17. Office of the Bosnian Serbs (Washington, D.C.)

18. The *New York Times* (N.Y.C.)
19. CRICINFO (London, England)/Ronald Hutton, Bristol University (Bristol, England)
20. Bundes Ministerium für Wirtschaft/Bundes Umwelt Ministerium (Bonn, Germany)
21. Associated Press (Paris, France)

22, 23. Polizei Präsidium (Bonn, Germany)

24. Paris Police Department
25. Cryodon Council (London, England)
26. The *Times of London*
27. British Broadcasting Service (London, England)
28. Association of the Independent Electronic Media (Belgrade, Republic of Serbia)
29. Ministry of the Environment (Oslo, Norway)
30. The British Weights and Measures System (Edinburgh, Scotland)
31. British Standards Institution (London, England)
32. Embassy of the Republic of Croatia (Washington, D.C.)
33. Ashley Weinberg, University of Manchester (England)
34. Embassy of Germany (Washington, D.C.)
35. Alcoholics Anonymous World Service (N.Y.C.)
36. Waterwinkel (Amsterdam)
37. The Office for National Statistics (London, England)

38, 39. UK Conservative Party (London, England)

40. Mentor Medical Inc. (Santa Barbara, Calif.)
41. Embassy of Britain (Washington, D.C.)/British Information Services (N.Y.C.)
42. *The Sunday Times* (London, England)
43. Consulate General of Ireland (N.Y.C.)
44. *The Irish Times* (Dublin, Ireland)
45. 10 Downing Street (London, England)
46. Das Deutsche Gartenzwerg Museum (Weisbaden, Germany)
47. Polish Press Agency (Warsaw, Poland)
48. British Nuclear Fuels (Warrington, England)

49, 50. Victor Lebre, Maison du Lac (Arles, France)

51. Mayor's Office (Paris, France)

LATIN AMERICA AND THE CARIBBEAN

1. Institute for Policy Studies (Washington, D.C.)

2–4. Instituto Nacional de Estadistica, Geografia e Informatica (Mexico City)/Federal Reserve Bank of Dallas (El Paso, Tex.)

5. Alexis de Tocqueville Institution (Arlington, Va.)

6. Cuban Interest Section, U.S. Department of State (Washington, D.C.)
7. Office of Cuban Affairs, U.S. Department of State (Washington, D.C.)
8. Reuters News Service (São Paulo, Brazil)
9. Comissão Pastoral da Terra (Goiânia, Brazil)
10. Washington Office on Latin America (Washington, D.C.)
11. Conseil Electoral Provisoire (Port-au-Prince, Haiti)/Embassy of Haiti (Washington, D.C.)
12. Embassy of Haiti (Washington, D.C.)
13. Instituto Federal Electoral (Mexico City)/U.S. Census Bureau (Washington, D.C.)
14. Washington Office on Latin America (Washington, D.C.)
15. Gideon Lichfield, Chief Correspondent, *The Economist* (Mexico City)
16. Embassy of Haiti (Washington, D.C.)
17. The White House (Washington, D.C.)
18. Embassy of Haiti (Washington, D.C.)
19. Latin America Working Group (Washington, D.C.)
20. World Health Organization/U.S. Department of Agriculture (Washington, D.C.)
21. Pan-American Health Organization (Washington, D.C.)
22. The National Center for Health Statistics (Hyattsville, Md.)
23. David E. Lorey, *The Rise of the Professions in Twentieth-Century Mexico*, UCLA Latin American Center Publications (Los Angeles)
24. *Reforma* (Mexico City)
25. Embassy of Mexico (Washington, D.C.)
26. U.S. Department of State (Washington, D.C.)
27. Fundacion Pais Libre (Bogota, Colombia)
28. Rafael Ruiz Harrell, National University of Mexico (Mexico City)
29. Procuraduria General de las Repúblíca (Mexico City)
30. Civil Engineering Department, Texas A&M University (College Station, Tex.)

MIGRATION

1. Robson Bonnichsen, Oregon State University (Corvallis)
2. Statue of Liberty–Ellis Island Foundation (N.Y.C.)

3, 4. Fred Rose, *Wall Street Journal* (Los Angeles)
5. U.S. Census Bureau (Washington, D.C.)
6. Choice Hotels International (Silver Spring, Md.)

7. UNICEF (N.Y.C.)
8–10. United Nations High Commissioner for Refugees (N.Y.C.)
11. Central Council of German Jews (Frankfurt, Germany)
12. Brenda Brasher, Mount Union College (Alliance, Ohio)
13. Central Statistics Office of Ireland (Dublin)
14–16. U.S. Immigration and Naturalization Service (Washington, D.C.)
17. Federal Bureau of Prisons (Washington, D.C.)
18. Karl Eschbach, University of Houston (Texas)
19. Texas A&M University (College Station, Tex.)/California Department of Food and Agriculture (Sacramento)
20. Peter Vitousek, Stanford University (Palo Alto, Calif.)
21. David Pimentel, Cornell University (Ithaca, N.Y.)
22. U.S. Census Bureau (Washington, D.C.)

TRANSPORTATION

1. National Sleep Foundation (Washington, D.C.)
2. *New England Journal of Medicine* (Boston)
3. Infrastructure Technology Institute (Evanston, Ill.)
4. U.S. Department of Transportation (Washington, D.C.)
5. Scott Hodge (Alexandria, Va.)/Technic, Inc. (Cranston, R.I.)
6. A-Aviara Limousine Service (Carlsbad, Calif.)
7. California Highway Patrol (Oceanside)
8. California Air Resources Board (Los Angeles)
9. Campbell Soup Company (Camden, N.J.)
10. U.S. Department of Energy (Albuquerque, N.Mex.)
11. Truckstop Ministries (Atlanta)
12. American Motorcyclist Association (Westerville, Ohio)
13. American Society for Microbiology (Washington, D.C.)
14, 15. Federal Aviation Administration (Washington, D.C.)
16. Congressional Research Service (Washington, D.C.)
17. Institute of Medicine (Washington, D.C.)
18. Zurich Municipal (Bournemouth, England)
19. AAA Foundation for Traffic Safety (Washington, D.C.)
20. U.S. Department of Transportation (Washington, D.C.)
21, 22. Detroit Department of Transportation
23. Office of Budget and Performance, U.S. Department of Transportation (Washington, D.C.)
24, 25. *Commuting in America*, Eno Transportation Foundation (Washington, D.C.)
26, 27. Internal Revenue Service (Washington, D.C.)
28. *Multinational Monitor* (Washington, D.C.)

29. Stockholm County Council (Sweden)
30. British Information Services (N.Y.C.)
31. Embassy of Brazil (Washington, D.C.)

32, 33. J. D. Power and Associates (Troy, Mich.)

34, 35. Ward's Communications Intertech Publishing (Southfield, Mich.)

36. Chuck Pillon (May Valley, Wash.)
37. U.S. Department of Transportation Semiannual Report to Congress, 1998 (Washington, D.C.)
38. Metropolitan Transit Authority (Los Angeles)/National Aeronautics and Space Administration (Washington, D.C.)

AMERICAN PIE

1. American Civil Liberties Union (Oklahoma City)
2. Q&A Consulting, Inc. (North Manchester, Ind.)
3. John B. Rae, *The Road and the Car in American Life*, MIT Press (Cambridge, Mass.)
4. James Reston Jr., *The Last Apocalypse*, Doubleday (N.Y.C.)
5. Ronald Takaki, University of California at Berkeley
6. California Governor's Office of Emergency Services (Sacramento)
7. Congressional Budget Office (Washington, D.C.)
8. Organisation for Economic Co-Operation and Development (Paris, France)

9, 10. Federal Reserve Board (Washington, D.C.)

11. Ohio State University (Columbus)
12. Department of History, Trinity University (San Antonio)
13. *Hemp for Victory*, USDA Motion Picture Services Division (Washington, D.C.)

14, 15. Bureau of Justice Statistics (Washington, D.C.)

16. Independent Sector (Washington, D.C.)
17. World Trade Organization (Geneva, Switzerland)/Public Citizens' Global Trade Watch (Washington, D.C.)
18. American Bankers Association (Washington, D.C.)

19, 20. Federal Reserve Board/Federal Deposit Insurance Corporation (Washington, D.C.)

21. Congressional Budget Office (Washington, D.C.)/*Harper's* research
22. Pew Research Center for the People and the Press (Washington, D.C.)

23, 24. Environmental Working Group (Washington, D.C.)/Montana Human Rights Network (Helena)

25, 26. Roper Starch Worldwide (N.Y.C.)
27. Franklin Associates (Prairie Village, Kans.)
28, 29. T. Harry Williams, *Huey Long,* Random House (N.Y.C.)
30, 31. Violence Policy Center (Washington, D.C.)
32. Centers for Disease Control and Prevention (Atlanta)
33. Ihsan Bagby, Shaw University (Raleigh, N.C.)
34. Flagstar Companies, Inc. (Spartanburg, S.C.)
35, 36. Henry J. Kaiser Family Foundation (Menlo Park, Calif.)
37, 38. Mexican Consulate (N.Y.C.)/*Harper's* research
39. Louis Harris and Associates (N.Y.C.)
40. Bureau of Indian Affairs (Washington, D.C.)/Franklin Delano Roosevelt Library (Hyde Park, N.Y.)
41. H/K Communications (N.Y.C.)
42. Sazerac Company, Inc. (New Orleans)
43. Harry Wibisono, Spokane Community College (Washington)

NEW YORK, NEW YORK

1, 2. New York Civil Liberties Union (N.Y.C.)
3. New York City Police Department
4. Civilian Complaint Review Board (N.Y.C)
5. New York Civil Liberties Union (N.Y.C.)
6. Office of the District Attorney for New York County (N.Y.C.)
7. Deputy Commissioner of Public Information (N.Y.C.)
8. Emery, Cuti, Brinckerhoff and Abady (N.Y.C.)
9, 10. New York Civil Liberties Union (N.Y.C.)
11. Bellevue Hospital Center (N.Y.C.)
12. Brooklyn Museum of Art (N.Y.C.)
13. New York City Police Department
14. WWOR-TV (N.Y.C.)
15. United States Geological Survey, National Earthquake Information Center (Denver)
16. Con Edison (N.Y.C.)
17. Citizens' Committee for Children of New York (N.Y.C.)
18. New York Yankees (N.Y.C.)
19. Andrew Beveridge, Queens College (N.Y.C.)/U.S. Census Bureau (Washington, D.C.)
20. Economic Development Corporation (N.Y.C.)
21. Ronald M. Dragoon, Ben's Kosher Delis (Hicksville, N.Y.)
22. Astoria Federal Savings (Lake Success, N.Y.)
23. New Jersey Attorney General's Office (Trenton)
24. New York City Department of Parks and Recreation
25. New York City Department of Health

26. Nina Lannan Associates (N.Y.C.)
27. Statue of Liberty National Monument and Ellis Island (N.Y.C.)

GOING SOUTH

1. Tennessee State Clerk's Office (Nashville)
2, 3. Office of the Council Coordinator/Lincoln Yellow Cab Company/*State Journal-Register*/Department of Community Relations (Springfield, Ill.)
4. The Sentencing Project (Washington, D.C.)
5. Alabama Education Association (Montgomery)
6, 7. Office of the Chief of Police (Washington, D.C.)
8. National Center for Education Statistics (Washington, D.C.)
9, 10. Muscogee County School District (Columbus, Ga.)
11. Opelousas Police Department (Opelousas, La.)
12. City Attorney's Office (Orlando, Fla.)
13. Texas Department of Human Services (Austin)
14. North American Mission Board, Southern Baptist Convention (Alpharetta, Ga.)
15. New Orleans Mosquito and Termite Control Board
16. Atlanta Regional Commission
17. Highway Safety Research Center, University of North Carolina (Chapel Hill)
18. Design Center (Little Rock, Ark.)
19. On A Roll, Inc. (Charlotte, N.C.)
20. U.S. Fish and Wildlife Service (Washington, D.C.)
21. Union Hill Cumberland Presbyterian Church (Athens, Ala.)
22. Office of the State Attorney General (Jackson, Miss.)

COMMUNICATIONS

NEWS

1, 2. The Newseum (Arlington, Va.)
3. The *Washington Post* (Washington, D.C.)
4, 5. Rocky Mountain Media Watch (Denver)
6. *Editor & Publisher*-Technometrica Policy and Politics poll (Emerson, N.J.)
7, 8. Libel Defense Resource Center (N.Y.C.)
9, 10. Center for the Advancement of Modern Media (Miami)
11. Johns Hopkins University (Baltimore)/PR Watch (Madison, Wis.)
12. *Harper's* research
13, 14. The Pew Research Center for the People and the Press (Washington, D.C.)

15, 16. The Gallup Organization (Princeton, N.J.)
    17. United Press International (Washington, D.C.)
    18. ADT Research (N.Y.C.)
    19. Russian Research Center (Cambridge, Mass.)
    20. The *New York Times* (Moscow, Russia)
    21. First Lady's Press Office (Washington, D.C.)
    22. *Harper's* research
    23. Atlante Star Hotel (Rome, Italy)
    24. CBS News (N.Y.C.)
    25. Ohio State University School of Journalism (Columbus)

THE TUBE

1. *America's Most Wanted* (Washington, D.C.)
2. Nielsen Media Research (N.Y.C.)
3. Nielsen Media Research (N.Y.C.)/ U.S. Office of Management and Budget (Washington, D.C.)
4, 5. Nielsen Media Research (N.Y.C.)
6. KRC Research and Consulting (N.Y.C.)
7. Federal Communications Commission (Washington, D.C.)/Nielsen Media Research (N.Y.C.)
8. The *New York Times* (N.Y.C.)
9. C-SPAN (Washington, D.C.)
10. PBS Corporate Information (Alexandria, Va.)/Corporation for Public Broadcasting (Washington, D.C.)
11. NBC (Los Angeles)/ABC (N.Y.C.)/CBS (Los Angeles)/*The Complete Directory to Prime Time Network and Cable TV Shows 1946–Present*, Ballantine Books (N.Y.C.)
12, 13. Pew Research Center for the People and the Press (Washington, D.C.)
14. TN Media, Inc. (N.Y.C.)
15. The Henry J. Kaiser Family Foundation (Menlo Park, Calif.)
16. U.S. Consumer Product Safety Commission (Washington, D.C.)
17. Motion Picture Screen Cartoonists, Local 839 (North Hollywood, Calif.)
18, 19. Harvard Eating Disorders Center (Boston)
20. Pearson Television (N.Y.C.)
21. International Broadcasting Bureau (Washington, D.C.)
22. QVC (West Chester, Pa.)
23. Office of Representative Rush Holt (Kingston, N.J.)
24. Saban Entertainment (Los Angeles)

HOLLYWOOD

1. *Harper's* research
2. The *New York Times* (N.Y.C.)
3. Paramount Pictures/RMS Titanic, Inc. (N.Y.C.)
4. National Endowment for the Arts (Washington, D.C.)/Internet Movie Database (http://www.imdb.com)
5. *Variety* (N.Y.C.)/Military Department, Emergency Management Division (Olympia, Wash.)
6. Artisan Entertainment/Dreamworks SKG (Los Angeles)
7. *Variety* (Los Angeles)
8, 9. Ziegfeld Theatre (N.Y.C.)
10. Office of Representative Robert Dornan (Washington, D.C.)/Motion Picture & TV Photo Archives (Van Nuys, Calif.)
11. Schwartz Public Relations (N.Y.C.)
12, 13. *People Weekly 1999 Entertainment Almanac*, Cader Books (N.Y.C.)
14. Cari Beauchamp, *Without Lying Down: Frances Marion and the Powerful Women of Early Hollywood*, Charles Scribner's Sons (N.Y.C.)
15. *Entertainment Weekly* (N.Y.C.)
16. Telecine Inc. (South Barrington, Ill.)
17. Christie's (N.Y.C.)
18. Jack G. Shaheen (Hilton Head, S.C.)
19. *Harper's* research
20. C-SPAN (Washington, D.C.)
21. Motion Picture Association of America (Washington, D.C.)
22. U.S. Bureau of Labor Statistics (Washington, D.C.)
23. The Walt Disney Corporation (Burbank, Calif.)
24. Mounted Police Foundation (Ottawa, Ontario)
25. Chuck LeFever (Los Angeles)

MUSIC

1. Recording Industry Association of America (Washington, D.C.)
2. POLLSTAR (Fresno, Calif.)/STEP Entertainment Services, Inc. (Toronto, Ontario)
3. David Fishof Presents (N.Y.C.)
4. Dean Witter Discover Card & Co. (Riverwoods, Ill.)
5. D.T.F. Co. (Raleigh, N.C.)
6. Neil Strauss (N.Y.C.)
7. WJMP (Akron, Ohio)
8. Kamaka Hawaii, Inc. (Honolulu)
9. Yehudi Menuhin, *Unfinished Journey*, Fromm International (N.Y.C.)

10. Consulting Radiologists Limited (Minneapolis)
11. Victoria's Secret (Columbus, Ohio)
12. Office of Senator Orrin Hatch (Washington, D.C.)
13. Pat Boone Enterprises (Los Angeles)
14. Soundata (White Plains, N.Y.)
15. Double XXposure, Inc. (N.Y.C.)
16. Recording Industry Association of America (Washington, D.C.)
17. Intercontinental Absurdities Ltd. (Los Angeles)
18. The White House (Washington, D.C.)
19. The Richard Nixon Presidential Library and Birthplace (Yorba Linda, Calif.)
20. Office of Senator Robert Dole (Washington, D.C.)

READING AND WRITING

1. Colonial Williamsburg (Va.)
2. John McCain, *Faith of My Fathers*, Random House/George W. Bush, *A Charge to Keep*, William Morrow & Company (N.Y.C.)
3. The American Poetry and Literacy Project (Washington, D.C.)
4. Angus Reid Group, Inc. (Ottawa, Ontario)
5. Karen Gillette, Foothill College (Los Altos, Calif.)
6. Boston Public Library
7. American Federation of State, County and Municipal Employees (Washington, D.C.)
8. Library of Congress (Washington, D.C.)
9. Gretchen Edgen, *The Playmate Book*, General Publishing Group (Santa Monica, Calif.)
10, 11. Omaha Public Library (Nebr.)
12. *Harper's* research
13. W. H. Bond and Hugh Amory, *The Printed Catalogues of the Harvard College Library*, Oak Knoll Press (Boston)
14. Fritz J. Raddatz, ed.,*The Marx-Engels Correspondence*, Wiedenfield & Nicolson (London, England)
15. *Talk* (N.Y.C.)
16. Baen Books (Riverdale, N.Y.)
17, 18. Lauriat's Bookstore (Boston)
19, 20. U.S. Naval Institute (Annapolis, Md.)
21. Egyptian General Book Organization (Cairo, Egypt)
22. Joseph Pereira (Boston)
23. Hasbro, Inc. (East Longmeadow, Mass.)
24, 25. *Cosmopolitan* (Moscow, Russia)
26. PEN American Center (N.Y.C.)

27. United Nations Population Division (Washington, D.C.)
28. Poetry Society (London, England)
29, 30. U.S. Patent and Trademark Office (Arlington, Va.)
31, 32. Sarah Bednarz, et al., *Build Our Nation*, Houghton Mifflin (Boston)
33, 34. Washington, D.C. Department of Corrections
35. Merriam-Webster Inc. (Springfield, Mass.)
36. Random House Reference & Information Publishing (N.Y.C.)
37. Picador (London, England)

IN THE MAIL

1. BAIGlobal Inc. Mail Monitor (Tarrytown, N.Y.)
2. U.S. Department of Defense (Washington, D.C.)
3, 4. Republican Senatorial Campaign Committee (Washington, D.C.)
5, 6. Philip Coughter, spokesperson for Linda Tripp (Washington, D.C.)
7. World Canine Freestyle Organization (Brooklyn, N.Y.)
8. Christian Tattoo Association (Willmar, Minn.)
9, 10. Los Angeles County Coroner
11. Sotheby's (N.Y.C.)
12. Gallery of History, Inc. (Las Vegas)
13, 14. *Dr. Quinn, Medicine Woman* (Agoura, Calif.)
15. Hallmark Cards (Kansas City, Mo.)

ON THE WIRE

1. Federal Communications Commission (Washington, D.C.)
2. American Association for the Advancement of Science/U.S. Census Bureau (Washington, D.C.)/NYNEX (N.Y.C.)
3. Taliban Islamic Mission (N.Y.C.)
4. James Gleick, *Faster*, Pantheon Books (N.Y.C.)
5. VirtualJerusalem.com (Jerusalem)
6. American Public Communications Council (Alexandria, Va.)/U.S. Department of Justice (Washington, D.C.)
7. New York State Department of Correctional Services (Albany)
8. http://www.1800autopsy.com
9. Cyber Dialogue (N.Y.C.)
10. PursuitWatch Network (San Dimas, Calif.)
11, 12. Call of the Wind (Ventura, Calif.)
13. Center for On-Line Addiction (Bradford, Pa.)
14. America's Health Network (Orlando, Fla.)
15. PoliticsOnline (Charleston, S.C.)
16. Common Cause (Washington, D.C.)
17, 18. The Technology Front (Westford, Mass.)

19. U.S. Department of Defense (Washington, D.C.)
20. China.com Corporation (Hong Kong)/Network Solutions (Herndon, Va.)
21. Article 19 (London, England)
22. The Learning Company (Cambridge, Mass.)
23. Federal Communications Commission (Washington, D.C.)
24. Counter Spy Shop (Washington, D.C.)
25. Miller Brewing Company (Milwaukee)

TALK

1–4. U.S. Census Bureau (Washington, D.C.)
5, 6. Modern Language Association (N.Y.C.)
7. Jared Diamond, *Guns, Germs, and Steel,* W. W. Norton & Company (N.Y.C.)
8. *Oxford English Dictionary,* Oxford University Press (Oxford, England)
9. Rosina Lippi-Green, Western Washington University (Bellingham)
10. Professional Voice Care Center (Hicksville, N.Y.)
11. Tupperware Corporation (Orlando, Fla.)
12. Office of Senator Robert Byrd (Washington, D.C.)
13. Annenberg Public Policy Center (Philadelphia)
14. *Harper's* research
15, 16. Annenberg Public Policy Center (Philadelphia)
17, 18. The Pew Research Center for the People and the Press (Washington, D.C.)
19. George W. Bush Presidential Exploratory Committee (Austin, Tex.)
20. Bill Bradley for President (West Orange, N.J.)/Clinton 2000 (N.Y.C.)/Office of the Governor (Albany, N.Y.)
21. *Talkers Magazine* (Longmeadow, Mass.)
22. Philips Consumer Electronics Co. (Atlanta)
23. Nickelodeon/Yankelovich Youth Monitor Study (N.Y.C.)
24. National Action Network (N.Y.C.)
25. Albrecht Folsing, *Albert Einstein: A Biography,* Penguin (London, England)

ECONOMICS

WEALTH AND POVERTY

1. United Nations Human Development Report 1998 (N.Y.C.)
2. Organization for Economic Cooperation and Development (Paris, France)

3. Edward N. Wolff, New York University (N.Y.C.)
4. Congressional Budget Office (Washington, D.C.)
5, 6. Center on Budget and Policy Priorities (Washington, D.C.)
7. Citizens for Tax Justice (Washington, D.C.)
8. Institute for Policy Studies/Investor Responsibility Research Center (Washington, D.C.)
9. Yankelovich Partners (Norwalk, Conn.)
10, 11. New York Office of Temporary and Disability Assistance (Albany, N.Y.)
12, 13. American Bankruptcy Institute (Alexandria, Va.)
14, 15. *Harper's* research
16. Pew Research Center for the People and the Press (Washington, D.C.)
17. The White House Press Office (Washington, D.C.)
18. Food and Nutrition Service/Food Stamp Program (Alexandria, Va.)
19. *Forbes* (N.Y.C.)
20, 21. J. Bradford DeLong, University of California at Berkeley
22. World Bank Group (Washington, D.C.)
23. Kevin Bales, *Disposable People: New Slavery in the Global Economy*, University of California Press (Berkeley)

TAXES

1, 2. Internal Revenue Service (Washington, D.C.)
3. U.S. Census Bureau (Washington, D.C.)
4, 5. Tax Foundation (Washington, D.C.)
6. Citizens for Tax Justice (Washington, D.C.)
7. Center on Budget and Policy Priorities (Washington, D.C.)
8. Citizens for Tax Justice (Washington, D.C.)
9. U.S. Office of Management and Budget/Internal Revenue Service (Washington, D.C.)/*Left Business Observer* (N.Y.C.)
10, 11. Internal Revenue Service (Washington, D.C.)
12. Joint Committee on Taxation (Washington, D.C.)
13. Senate Finance Committee (Washington, D.C.)
14, 15. Citizens for Tax Justice (Washington, D.C.)
16. Manpower International Inc. (Milwaukee)/*Ward's Business Directory of U.S. Private and Public Companies*, Gale Group (Farmington Hills, Mich.)
17, 18. Internal Revenue Service (Washington, D.C.)
19. Senate Budget Committee (Washington, D.C.)
20. Internal Revenue Service (Washington, D.C.)
21. The Center for Public Integrity (Washington, D.C.)/Sanford and Associates (Dallas)
22. Office of the Speaker of the House (Washington, D.C.)

IOUS

1. Jonathan Drimmer (Washington, D.C.)
2. Administrative Office of the U.S. Courts (Washington, D.C.)
3. National Foundation for Consumer Credit (Silver Spring, Md.)
4. North American Securities Administrators Association, Inc. (Washington, D.C.)
5–7. U.S. Department of Justice (Washington, D.C.)
8. CardWeb.com (Frederick, Md.)
9. American Bankers Association (Washington, D.C.)
10. U.S. Department of Agriculture (Washington, D.C.)
11, 12. House Committee on Government Reform and Health Oversight/Minerals Management Service (Washington, D.C.)
13. United Nations (N.Y.C.)/U.S. Department of State (Washington, D.C.)
14, 15. United Nations (N.Y.C.)
16. Korean Ministry of Finance and Economy (Seoul)
17, 18. Japan Economic Institute (Washington, D.C.)
19, 20. World Bank (Washington, D.C.)
21. *Harper's* research
22, 23. Office of Management and Budget (Washington, D.C.)
24, 25. Health Resources and Services Administration (Washington, D.C.)
26. Goodfellow Rebecca Ingrams Pearson (London, England)
27. Visa/PLUS ATM Network (San Francisco)
28, 29. Associated Press (Moscow, Russia)

IMPORTS AND EXPORTS

1. Wirthlin Worldwide (McLean, Va.)/Federal Election Commission (Washington, D.C.)
2, 3. Global Trade Watch (Washington, D.C.)
4, 5. International Forum on Globalization (San Francisco)
6. World Policy Institute (N.Y.C.)/Federation of American Scientists (Washington, D.C.)
7. William Kirby, Harvard University (Cambridge, Mass.)
8, 9. Eric Hobsbawm, *The Age of Revolution*, Vintage (N.Y.C.)
10. U.S. Department of Commerce (Washington, D.C.)
11. U.S. Department of State (Washington, D.C.)
12. U.S. Census Bureau (Washington, D.C.)
13, 14. U.S. Department of Agriculture (Washington, D.C.)
15. U.S. Census Bureau (Washington, D.C.)
16. National Conference of Catholic Bishops (Washington, D.C.)
17. Mariage Freres (Paris, France)

18. U.S. Department of Agriculture (Washington, D.C.)
19. Shanghai Tang (N.Y.C.)
20. Amway Corporation (Ada, Mich.)
21. Victorinox (Ibach, Switzerland)/Wenger S.A. (Delemont, Switzerland)

SPECULATION

1. Economic Policy Institute (Washington, D.C.)
2. *Forbes* (N.Y.C.)
3. Groucho Marx, *Groucho and Me*, B. Geis Associates (N.Y.C.)
4. Edward Chancellor, *Devil Take the Hindmost*, Farrar, Straus and Giroux (N.Y.C.)
5. Dole-Kemp '96 (Washington, D.C.)
6, 7. Comedy Central (N.Y.C.)
8. Perot Systems Corporation (Dallas)
9. Lippert/Heilshorn Inc. (N.Y.C.)
10, 11. Stapleton Communications Inc. (Mountain View, Calif.)/*Wall Street Journal* (N.Y.C.)
12. National Gambling Impact Study Commission (Washington, D.C.)
13. North American Association of State and Provincial Lotteries (Cleveland)
14. U.S. Department of the Treasury (Washington, D.C.)
15. David P. Phillips, University of California at San Diego (La Jolla, Calif.)
16. The Center for Public Integrity (Washington, D.C.)
17. U.S. Census Bureau (Washington, D.C.)
18, 19. Thomas A. Watts-Fitzgerald, Assistant U.S. Attorney (Miami)
20, 21. *Harper's* research
22. The John F. Kennedy School of Government, Harvard University (Cambridge, Mass.)
23, 24. Hal Brill, Jack A. Brill, and Cliff Feigenbaum, *Investing With Your Values*, Bloomberg Press (Princeton, N.J.)
25, 26. Investor Responsibility Research Center (Washington, D.C.)
27, 28. *Left Business Observer* (N.Y.C.)
29, 30. New York University Downtown Hospital (N.Y.C.)
31. Dow Jones & Company, Inc. (N.Y.C.)
32. Guinness World Records (London, England)

THE CORPORATE WORLD

1. Society for Human Resource Management (Alexandria, Va.)
2. Society of Competitive Intelligence Professionals (Alexandria, Va.)

3. Microsoft (Redmond, Wash.)
4. The Center for Responsive Politics (Washington, D.C.)
5. House Committee on Commerce (Washington, D.C.)
6. Dow Jones & Company (N.Y.C.)
7. U.S. Department of Justice (Washington, D.C.)
8. Embassy of France (Washington, D.C.)/America Online (Sterling, Va.)
9, 10. Viacom Inc. (N.Y.C.)/*Harper's* research
11. Corporation for Public Broadcasting (Washington, D.C.)
12, 13. International Events Group (Chicago)
14. Team Marketing Report, Inc. (Chicago)
15. Charles W. Thomas, Center for Studies in Criminology and Law (Gainesville, Fla.)
16. New York Life (N.Y.C.)
17. eToys, Inc. (Santa Monica, Calif.)
18. Wisconsin Department of Workforce Development (Madison)
19. *Fortune* (N.Y.C.)
20. American Management Association (N.Y.C.)
21, 22. Cynthia Kisser, former director, Cult Awareness Network (Wonder Lake, Ill.)
23, 24. Rat Paradise (Encinitas, Calif.)
25. Ralph Nader (Washington, D.C.)

ON THE JOB

1. American Association for Marriage and Family Therapy (Washington, D.C.)
2, 3. International Facility Management Association (Houston, Tex.)
4. Senate Permanent Subcommittee on Investigations (Washington, D.C.)
5. Samuel Dash, Georgetown University Law School (Washington, D.C.)
6. U.S. Department of Justice (Washington, D.C.)
7, 8. Office of Representative Richard Gephardt (Washington, D.C.)
9–11. U.S. Department of Labor (Washington, D.C.)
12, 13. *New York Times* poll (N.Y.C.)
14. Organization for International Investment (Washington, D.C.)
15. U.S. Census Bureau (Washington, D.C.)
16, 17. The *Washington Post*–Kaiser Family Foundation–Harvard University Survey Project/U.S. Department of Labor (Washington, D.C.)
18. Bureau of Labor Statistics (Washington, D.C.)

19. Challenger, Gray & Christmas, Inc. (Chicago)
20. General Accounting Office (Washington, D.C.)
21, 22. Office of Management and Budget/U.S. Office of Personnel Management (Washington, D.C.)
23–26. Bureau of Labor Statistics (Washington, D.C.)
27. Economic Policy Institute (Washington, D.C.)
28. Robert Pollin and Stephanie Luce, *The Living Wage*, New Press (N.Y.C.)
29. Bureau of Labor Statistics (Washington, D.C.)
30, 31. Disney World (Orlando, Fla.)
32. Bureau of Labor Statistics (Washington, D.C.)
33. Research Center for Arts and Culture, Columbia University (N.Y.C.)
34. National Public Radio (Washington, D.C.)
35. VA News Service (Washington, D.C.)
36. U.S. Census Bureau (Washington, D.C.)/Wal-Mart (Bentonville, Ark.)
37. Michigan Department of Commerce/Michigan Department of Education (Lansing)
38. New York Department of State (Albany)
39. New York State Department of Health (Albany)
40. New York City Department of Social Services
41. Medieval Times (Lyndhurst, N.J.)
42. Waggener-Edstrom (Portland, Ore.)

SHOPPING

1. Mall of America (Bloomington, Minn.)
2. Roper Starch Worldwide (N.Y.C)
3. ArtRock Gallery (San Francisco)
4. Mattel, Inc. (El Segundo, Calif.)
5. National Labor Committee (Washington, D.C.)
6. *Correctional Industries Association Directory 1998* (Baltimore)
7. Kmart Resource Center (Troy, Mich.)/Center for Defense Information (Washington, D.C.)
8, 9. Center for Defense Information/General Accounting Office (Washington, D.C.)
10. Malcolm Kushner and Associates (Santa Cruz, Calif.)
11. Nate's Autographs (Los Angeles)
12. Wayne Lensing (Rockford, Ill.)
13. MPI Media Group (Orland Park, Ill.)/National Archives (Washington, D.C.)
14, 15. *Worth* (N.Y.C.)

16. Diana, Princess of Wales Memorial Fund (London, England)

17, 18. Office of the Governor (Tallahassee, Fla.)

19. Nine West Group Inc. (White Plains, N.Y.)

20. U.S. Atomic Museum (Albuquerque, N. Mex.)

21. Alaska State Chemistry Laboratory (Juneau)

22. Fox News/Opinion Dynamics poll (N.Y.C.)

23. Merck Family Fund (Takoma Park, Md.)

SCIENCE

TECHNOLOGY

1. Massachusetts Institute of Technology Leg Lab (Cambridge)

2. Jaguar North America (Mahwah, N.J.)

3. U.S. Department of Transportation (Washington, D.C.)

4. Maine Bureau of Motor Vehicles (Augusta)

5. Department of Public Works (Los Angeles)

6. Solace Consultancy Services (Bexhill on Sea, East Sussex, England)

7. International Y2K Cooperation Center (Washington, D.C.)

8. Office of Management and Budget (Washington, D.C.)

9, 10. National Center for Supercomputing Applications (Champaign-Urbana, Ill.)

11. U.S. Army Simulation Training and Instrumentation Command (Orlando, Fla.)

12. DigiPen Institute of Technology (Redmond, Wash.)

13. Northlich Stolley LaWarre–Techtel Corporation poll (Cincinnati)

14. *Harper's* research

15. Ampro Electronics, Inc. (Santa Monica, Calif.)

16. Avon Silversmiths Ltd. (Bishop's Stortford, England)

17, 18. U.S. Patent and Trademark Office (Arlington, Va.)

19, 20. Susan Jonas and Marilyn Nissenson, *Going, Going, Gone,* Chronicle Books (San Francisco)

21. U.S. Patent and Trademark Office (Washington, D.C.)

OUTER SPACE

1. Celestis Inc. (Houston, Tex.)

2. U.S. Department of Defense (Arlington, Va.)

3. U.S. Space Command (Colorado Springs, Colo.)

4. Los Alamos National Laboratory (Los Alamos, N. Mex.)

5. Joseph Burns, Cornell University (Ithaca, N.Y.)

6. National Center for Atmospheric Research (Boulder, Colo.)

7. National Aeronautics and Space Administration (Washington, D.C.)

8. Chicago Academy of Sciences
9. William Welch, University of California at Berkeley
10. Fox News/Opinion Dynamics poll (N.Y.C.)
11. Elvis Presley Enterprises (Memphis)/National Aeronautics and Space Administration (Washington, D.C.)
12. Angus Reid Group, Inc. (Ottawa, Ontario)
13. Mattel, Inc. (El Segundo, Calif.)
14. Johnson Space Center (Houston, Tex.)
15. Minor Planet Center (Cambridge, Mass.)
16. Kennedy Space Center (Cape Canaveral, Fla.)
17. Marshall Space Center (Huntsville, Ala.)
18. Nielsen Media Research (N.Y.C.)
19. National Aeronautics and Space Administration (Washington, D.C.)
20. Space Telescope Science Institute (Baltimore)
21. Christopher Anderson, University of Wisconsin (Madison)
22. Michio Kaku, City College of New York (N.Y.C.)

WEATHER CONDITIONS

1–3. The Weather Channel (Atlanta)
4. U.S. Department of Agriculture (Washington, D.C.)
5. Interstate Commission on the Potomac River Basin (Rockville, Md.)
6, 7. Insurance Services Office, Inc. (N.Y.C)
8. Insurance Services Office, Inc. (N.Y.C)/U.S. Census Bureau (Washington, D.C.)
9, 10. National Climatic Data Center (Asheville, N.C.)
11, 12. Randall Cerveny, Arizona State University (Tempe)
13, 14. Department of Applied Physics, University of Santiago (Spain)
15. National Climatic Data Center (Asheville, N.C.)
16. Alfonso Niño (Pomono, Calif.)
17. Goddard Space Flight Center, National Aeronautics and Space Administration (Greenbelt, Md.)
18, 19. Worldwatch Institute (Washington, D.C.)
20. Coroner's Office, West London (England)
21. National Weather Service (Lincoln, Ill.)/Washington Park Botanical Gardens (Springfield, Ill.)
22. Thomas Stearns Eliot

REAPING AND SOWING

1. American Farmland Trust (Washington, D.C.)
2, 3. U.S. Department of Agriculture (Washington, D.C.)

4. National Institute on Drug Abuse/Food and Drug Administration (Rockville, Md.)
5. Foreign Agricultural Service, U.S. Department of Agriculture (Washington, D.C.)
6. International Trade Administration, U.S. Department of Commerce (Washington, D.C.)
7, 8. Bill Chameides, Georgia Institute of Technology (Atlanta)
9. University of Texas (Austin)
10. Felipe Fernández-Armesto, *Millennium: A History of the Last Thousand Years*, Touchstone (N.Y.C.)
11. Jared Diamond, *Guns, Germs, and Steel*, W. W. Norton & Company (N.Y.C.)
12. Vanilla, Saffron Imports (San Francisco)
13. European Commission (N.Y.C.)
14. McDonald's staff (Arles, France)
15. Duchy of Cornwall's Home Farm (Gloucestershire, England)
16. Consumers Union (N.Y.C.)
17. Department of Entomology, Michigan State University (East Lansing)
18. Biotechnology Industry Organization (Washington, D.C.)
19, 20. *The Ecologist* (London, England)
21, 22. Jane Akre (Clearwater, Fla.)
23. Thompson & Morgan (Jackson, N.J.)

THE ANIMAL KINGDOM

1. National Park Service (Washington, D.C.)
2–4. New Hampshire Fish and Game Department (Keene)
5. National Audobon Society (N.Y.C.)
6. Hong Kong Economic and Trade Bureau (Washington, D.C.)/KFC (Louisville, Ky.)
7. Western Monastery (Hong Kong)
8. National Turkey Federation (Washington, D.C.)
9. Pleasanton Superior Court (Pleasanton, Calif.)
10. U.S. Fish and Wildlife Service (Albuquerque, N.Mex.)
11, 12. Consulate General of Australia (N.Y.C.)
13. Roger Morse, Cornell University (Ithaca, N.Y.)
14. Yellowstone National Park (Wyo.)
15. National Bison Association (Denver)
16. American Emu Association (Dallas)
17. Performing Animal Welfare Society (Galt, Calif.)/People for the Ethical Treatment of Animals (Norfolk, Va.)
18. *Bee Culture* magazine (Medina, Ohio)

19. The Nature Conservancy (Providence, R.I.)
20. Herbert S. Terrace, Columbia University (N.Y.C.)
21. Daniel A. Potter, University of Kentucky (Lexington)
22. British Trust for Ornithology (London, England)
23. U.S. Office of Migratory Bird Management (Arlington, Va.)
24. Exxon Valdez Oil Spill Trustee Council (Anchorage, Alaska)
25. Stephen Keller, Yale University (New Haven, Conn.)
26. Ames Research Center (Moffett, Calif.)
27. U.S. Department of Agriculture (Washington, D.C.)
28. San Francisco Zoo
29. National Cancer Institute (Frederick, Md.)
30. U.S. Geological Survey Biological Resources Division, Pacific Island Ecosystems Research Center (Hawaii National Park)
31. National Science Foundation (Arlington, Va.)/*Sierra* magazine (San Francisco)
32. Embassy of Norway (Washington, D.C.)
33. KLM Airlines (Amsterdam)
34. Center for Marine Conservation (Washington, D.C.)
35. Oxford Museum of Natural History (Oxford, England)

THE ENVIRONMENT

1, 2. *Oil Spill Intelligence Report* (Arlington, Mass.)
3. World Resources Institute (Washington, D.C.)
4. Pond Action (Oxford, England)
5. The West Virginia Highlands Conservancy (Rockcabe, W.Va.)/U.S. Fish and Wildlife Service (Washington, D.C.)
6. NASA Goddard Space Flight Center (Greenbelt, Md.)
7. British Antarctic Survey (Cambridge, England)
8. Yanling Yu, University of Washington (Seattle)
9–11. British Antarctic Survey (Cambridge, England)
12. National Ice Center (Suitland, Md.)
13, 14. National Oceanic and Atmospheric Association (Boulder, Colo.)
15. Nancy Rabalais, Louisiana Universities Marine Consortium (Cocodrie, La.)
16. National Undersea Research Center (Groton, Conn.)
17. Global Coral Reef Alliance (Chappaqua, N.Y.)
18. Army Corps of Engineers (Mobile, Ala.)
19. Mississippi Beautification and Restoration Project (East Moline, Ill.)
20, 21. National Football League (N.Y.C.)
22. GrassRoots Recycling Network (Athens, Ga.)
23. City of Phoenix Planning Department (Arizona)
24. Wilderness Society (Washington, D.C.)

25. Public Research Works (Austin, Tex.)
26. Federal Emergency Management Agency (Washington, D.C.)
27. U.S. Department of Energy (Washington, D.C.)
28. League of Conservation Voters (Washington, D.C.)

ENERGY

1. U.S. Department of Energy (Washington, D.C.)/B & E Quality, Inc. (N.Y.C.)
2. United Space Alliance (Houston, Tex.)/Corel Corporation (Ottawa, Ontario)
3, 4. U.S. Environmental Protection Agency (Washington, D.C.)
5. Energy Information Administration (Washington, D.C.)
6. Regulatory Assistance Project (Montpelier, Vt.)
7, 8. Worldwatch Institute (Washington, D.C.)
9. BNFL (Cheshire, England)
10. Embassy of Ukraine (Washington, D.C.)/*Harper's* research
11, 12. Public Citizen (Washington, D.C.)
13. Nuclear Regulatory Commission (Washington, D.C.)
14, 15. U.S. Department of Energy (Washington, D.C.)
16, 17. Texas Transportation Institute (College Station)
18. *Harper's* research/Boeing Company (Seattle)
19. *Oil Spill Intelligence Report* (Arlington, Mass.)
20. New York State Department of Environmental Conservation (Albany)/*Harper's* research
21, 22. Alabama Department of Corrections (Montgomery)
23, 24. U.S. Department of Energy (Washington, D.C.)

GENETICS

1. Incyte Pharmaceuticals, Inc. (Palo Alto, Calif.)
2. Jackson Laboratory (Bar Harbor, Maine)
3. Monticello (Charlottesville, Va.)/The Starr Report
4. The Starr Report
5–7. Mannvernd, Association of Icelanders for Ethics in Science and Medicine (Reykjavic, Iceland)
8. Los Angeles Police Department
9. Texas A&M University (College Station, Tex.)
10. Encounter 2001 LLC (Houston, Tex.)
11. PPL Therapeutics (Edinburgh, Scotland)
12. The Wellcome Trust (London, England)
13. Fox News/Opinion Dynamics poll (N.Y.C.)
14. Barna Research Group (Ventura, Calif.)
15. New England Regional Genetics Group (Newton, Mass.)

HEALTH RISKS

1. National Center for Health Statistics (Hyattsville, Md.)
2. Stiletto Shoes (N.Y.C.)/American Podiatric Medical Association (Bethesda, Md.)/National Center for Health Statistics (Hyattsville, Md.)
3. Division of Research, Kaiser Permanente (Oakland, Calif.)
4. National Institute of Justice/Federal Bureau of Investigation (Washington, D.C.)
5. Sanford Institute of Public Policy (Durham, N.C.)
6. Centers for Disease Control and Prevention (Atlanta)/National Center for Health Statistics (Hyattsville, Md.)
7, 8. Fox News/Opinion Dynamics poll
9. *Roll Call* (Washington, D.C.)
10. Senate Democratic Policy Committee (Washington, D.C.)
11, 12. U.S. Health Care Financing Administration (Baltimore)
13, 14. New England Medical Center (Boston)
15, 16. The Henry J. Kaiser Family Foundation (Menlo Park, Calif.)
17. The Early Lung Cancer Action Program (N.Y.C.)
18, 19. Centers for Disease Control and Prevention/American Cancer Society (Atlanta)/*Harper's* research
20, 21. Leukemia Society of America (N.Y.C.)
22. U.S. Department of State (Washington, D.C.)
23. American Association for World Health (Washington, D.C.)
24–26. Centers for Disease Control and Prevention (Atlanta)
27, 28. Centers for Disease Control and Prevention (Atlanta)/Insurance Information Institute (N.Y.C.)
29. Statistical Information Department, U.S. Consumer Product Safety Commission (Silver Spring, Md.)
30. U.S. Food and Drug Administration (Rockville, Md.)
31. Charles Staggs (Stockton, Iowa)
32, 33. Duke University Medical Center (Raleigh-Durham, N.C.)/Centers for Disease Control and Prevention (Atlanta)
34. University of Michigan and Veterans' Administration Medical Center (Ann Arbor)
35. Judith Shindul-Rothschild, Boston College
36. Peter Sebel, Grady Memorial Hospital (Atlanta)

HEALTH CARE

1. *Annals of Internal Medicine* (Philadelphia)
2. Jan A. Staessen, MD, Ph.D. (Brussels, Belgium)
3. Governor's Task Force on Domestic and Sexual Violence (Tallahassee, Fla.)

4. Catholics for Free Choice (Washington, D.C.)
5. The Alan Guttmacher Institute (N.Y.C.)
6. The Council on Resident Education in Obstetrics and Gynecology (Washington, D.C.)
7. The Alan Guttmacher Institute (N.Y.C.)/Women's Research and Education Institute (Washington, D.C.)
8, 9. Kaiser Permanente (Oakland, Calif.)
10. National Conference of State Legislatures (Washington, D.C.)
11, 12. U.S. Department of Labor (Washington, D.C.)
13, 14. U.S. Census Bureau (Washington, D.C.)
15. Neil Wenger, UCLA School of Medicine (Los Angeles)
16. United Network for Organ Sharing (Richmond, Va.)
17. Hawaii Department of Health (Honolulu)
18. Hawaii Reference Bureau (Honolulu)
19, 20. Center for Studying Health System Change (Washington, D.C.)
21. Employee Benefit Research Institute (Washington, D.C.)
22. California Highway Patrol (San Francisco)

EPIDEMICS

1, 2. Jared Diamond, *Guns, Germs, and Steel*, W. W. Norton & Company (N.Y.C.)
3. UNAIDS (N.Y.C.)
4. *New England Journal of Medicine* (Boston)
5. *Archives of General Psychiatry* (N.Y.C.)
6. IMS HEALTH (Plymouth Meeting, Pa.)
7. ActUp (N.Y.C.)/World Bank (Washington, D.C.)
8. ActUp (N.Y.C.)
9. United Nations (N.Y.C.)
10. National Center for Infectious Diseases (Atlanta)
11–13. World Health Organization (Geneva, Switzerland)
14, 15. Edward Hooper, *The River*, Little, Brown and Company (N.Y.C.)
16–18. UNAIDS (N.Y.C.)
19. United Nations (N.Y.C.)
20. World Health Organization (Geneva, Switzerland)

PSYCHOLOGY

ANXIETY

1. Shyness Institute (Stanford, Calif.)
2. Substance Abuse and Mental Health Services Administration (Rockville, Md.)
3. Scott-Levin Associates (Newtown, Pa.)

4. Harvard School of Public Health (Cambridge, Mass.)
5. Louis Harris and Associates (N.Y.C.)
6, 7. CNN–*USA Today*–Gallup poll (Princeton, N.J.)
8. The Gallup Organization (Princeton, N.J.)
9. Stanard & Associates, Inc. (Chicago)
10, 11. North Carolina Office of the Appellate Defender (Durham)
12. The Nob Hill Lambourne (San Francisco)
13. Otis Elevator Company (Farmington, Conn.)
14. NBC–*Wall Street Journal* poll

NARCISSISM

1. Marin County Public Defender's Office (San Rafael, Calif.)
2. Louis Harris & Associates (N.Y.C.)
3. Goodfellow Rebecca Ingrams Pearson (London, England)
4. The *New York Times/WeightWatchers* magazine (N.Y.C.)
5. American Association of Blood Banks (Bethesda, Md.)
6. Naval Bureau of Medicine and Surgery (Washington, D.C.)
7. MTV (N.Y.C.)/Peace Corps (Washington, D.C.)
8. Leflein Associates (Fort Lee, N.J.)
9. *Harper's* research
10. Reed Larson, University of Illinois (Champaign-Urbana)

FEARS

1. Innovative Marketing Alliance (Dana Point, Calif.)
2. *USA Today* poll (Arlington, Va.)
3. Michael W. Cuneo, Fordham University (Bronx, N.Y.)
4. Dennis Turk, University of Washington School of Medicine (Seattle)
5, 6. Downtown Partnership of Baltimore
7, 8. Redwood City Police Department (Calif.)
9. National Association of Town Watch (Wynnewood, Pa.)
10. CAP Index (Exton, Pa.)
11. Luntz Research (Arlington, Va.)
12. *Adweek* (N.Y.C.)/Alden & Associates (Hermosa Beach, Calif.)
13. Susan Jonas and Marilyn Nissenson, *Going, Going, Gone*, Chronicle Books (San Francisco)
14. U.S. Federal Aviation Administration (Washington, D.C.)
15–17. U.S. Department of State (Washington, D.C.)

BELIEFS

1. Billy Graham Evangelistic Association (Minneapolis)
2. Yankelovich Partners (Claremont, Calif.)/Lutheran Brotherhood (Minneapolis)

3. The Salesian Sisters of St. John Bosco (North Haledon, N.J.)
4. Tyndale House (Carol Stream, Ill.)
5. Barna Research Group Ltd. (Glendale, Calif.)
6. *Le Monde* (Paris, France)
7, 8. Jon Man, *Atlas of the Year 1000,* Harvard University Press (Cambridge, Mass.)
9. Parents, Teachers & Students for Social Responsibility (Montpelier, Vt.)
10. American Gathering of Jewish Holocaust Survivors (N.Y.C.)/ Church of Jesus Christ of Latter-Day Saints (Salt Lake City)
11. North American Mission Board, Southern Baptist Convention (Alpharetta, Ga.)
12. *Newsweek* poll (N.Y.C.)
13, 14. Richard Day Research for Fidelity Investments (Boston)
15. *Congressional Record* (Washington, D.C.)
16. *Time* (N.Y.C.)
17. Fox News/Opinion Dynamics poll (N.Y.C.)
18, 19. The Preamble Society for Public Policy (Washington, D.C.)
20. Martin Luther King Jr. Library (Atlanta)
21. DuPage County State Attorney's Office (Wheaton, Ill.)/Office of Representative Newt Gingrich (Washington, D.C.)
22. CBS/*New York Times* poll (N.Y.C.)
23. The Alan Guttmacher Institute (N.Y.C.)
24. Pew Research Center for the People and the Press (Washington, D.C.)
25, 26. Sanofi Research (Great Valley, Pa.)
27. *Adweek* (N.Y.C.)/Alden & Associates (Hermosa Beach, Calif.)
28. *Nature* (Washington, D.C.)

HOME EC

MARRIED LIFE

1. *People* (N.Y.C.)
2. *Yakima Herald Republic* (Yakima, Wash.)
3. Princeton Survey Research Associates (Princeton, N.J.)
4. Roper Starch Worldwide (N.Y.C.)
5, 6. Bary Sinrod and Marlo Grey, *Just Married,* Andrews McMeel Publishing (Kansas City, Mo.)
7. Utah Legislature (Salt Lake City)
8. Bountiful County Police Department (Bountiful, Utah)
9. Alaska Public Offices Commission (Anchorage)
10. Assistant to the Ecclesiastical Delegate of the Holy See (Charleston, S.C.)

11. *Harper's* research
12. Office of Representative Barney Frank (Washington, D.C.)
13. Karen Foerstel, *Congressional Women,* Greenwood Press (Westport, Conn.)
14. National Center for Health Statistics (Hyattsville, Md.)
15, 16. Fox News/Opinion Dynamics poll (N.Y.C.)
17. National Center for Health Statistics (Hyattsville, Md.)
18. Bary Sinrod and Marlo Grey, *Just Married,* Andrews McMeel Publishing (Kansas City, Mo.)
19. *Divorce Magazine* (Toronto, Ontario)
20, 21. William Morris Agency (N.Y.C.)

MODERN BABY MAKING

1. Holbaek Hospital (Holbaek, Denmark)
2. Ambassador Artist Agency, Inc. (Nashville)
3. *The Lancet* (London, England)
4. Center for Human Reproduction (N.Y.C.)
5. Fenway Community Health Center (Boston)
6, 7. Human Fertilization and Embryology Authority (London, England)
8. Delaware Department of Justice (Wilmington)
9, 10. Women's Law Project (Philadelphia)
11, 12. U.S. Department of Health and Human Services (Washington, D.C.)
13. *Harper's* research
14, 15. Mike A. Males,*The Scapegoat Generation,* Common Courage Press/Child Trends, Inc. (Washington, D.C.)
16. The Russ Reid Company (Pasadena, Calif.)/Barna Research Group (Glendale, Calif.)
17. Centers for Disease Control and Prevention (Atlanta)
18. U.S. Department of Health and Human Services (Washington, D.C.)
19, 20. Social Security Administration (Baltimore)

FAMILY AFFAIRS

1. National Opinion Research Center, University of Chicago
2. Annie E. Casey Foundation (Baltimore)
3, 4. National Partnership for Women & Families (Washington, D.C.)
5. Chicago Legal Aid to Incarcerated Mothers
6, 7. National Abortion and Reproductive Rights Action League (Washington, D.C.)
8–11. Bureau of Justice Statistics (Washington, D.C.)
12. National Parent-Teacher Association (Chicago)/U.S. Department of Education (Washington, D.C.)
13. American Pet Association (Atlanta)

14. Office of Senator Strom Thurmond (Washington, D.C.)
15. United Press International poll (Washington, D.C.)
16. *Harper's* research
17. *People* (N.Y.C.)
18. Turner Broadcasting Network (Atlanta)
19. Statistical Research Inc. (Westfield, N.J.)
20. Robert Wood Johnson Foundation (Princeton, N.J.)

AROUND THE HOUSE

1, 2. Arthur Upgren, Wesleyan University (Middletown, Conn.)
   3. Ralph Lauren (N.Y.C.)
   4. Robert Rochon (Toronto, Ontario)
   5. Huron County Prosecuting Attorney (Bad Axe, Mich.)
   6. Lemelson–MIT Prize Program (Cambridge, Mass.)
   7. Waggener Edstrom (Portland, Oreg.)
   8. KRC Research & Consulting (N.Y.C.)
9–11. *Martha Stewart Living* (N.Y.C.)
   12. Environmental Protection Agency (Washington, D.C.)
   13. American Lawn Mower (Shelbyville, Ind.)
   14. Tiffany & Co. (N.Y.C.)
   15. *Organic Gardening* (Emmaus, Pa.)
   16. Nassau County Police Department (Mineola, N.Y.)
   17. Stanley Coren, University of British Columbia (Vancouver)
   18. Ivor Spencer International School for Butler Administrators and Personal Assistants/Aviation Corporation, Plc. (London, England)
   19. Century 21 Clemens & Sons Realty Inc. (Hartford, Conn.)
20–22. Felipe Fernández-Armesto, *Millennium: A History of the Last Thousand Years*, Touchstone (N.Y.C.)

EDIBLES AND POTABLES

   1. Jeffrey Steingarten, *Vogue* (N.Y.C.)
   2. Grocery Manufacturers of America (Washington, D.C.)
   3. Hormel Foods Corporation (Austin, Minn.)
4, 5. Pillsbury Corporation (Minneapolis)
   6. Miller Brewing Company (Milwaukee)
   7. Scribner Publishing (N.Y.C.)
   8. Food and Agriculture Organization of the United Nations (Rome, Italy)
   9. Worldwatch Institute (Washington, D.C.)
   10. Whale Product Analysis Study (San Francisco)
   11. Royal Society for the Prevention of Accidents (Birmingham, England)

12. Impact Databank (N.Y.C.)
13, 14. Bureau of Labor Statistics (Washington, D.C.)
15. McNeil Specialty Products (New Brunswick, N.J.)
16, 17. *American Journal of Clinical Nutrition* (Bethesda, Md.)
18, 19. Stanford Medical Center (Palo Alto, Calif.)
20. Connecticut Department of Public Health and Addiction Services (Hartford)
21. U.S. Department of Agriculture (Washington, D.C.)
22. Diet Dirt Excavations (Deerfield, Ill.)
23. American Association of Poison Control Centers (Washington, D.C.)

SHELTER

1. Consulate of Japan (N.Y.C.)/Inspections Unlimited (Philadelphia)
2. National Association of Home Builders (Washington, D.C.)
3. Mediamark Research Inc. (N.Y.C.)
4. University of Calgary (Alberta)
5. Susan Jonas and Marilyn Nissenson, *Going, Going, Gone*, Chronicle Books (San Francisco)
6. National Fire Protection Association (Quincy, Mass.)
7. Bill Sprout (Ennis, Mont.)
8. Federal Bureau of Investigation (Washington, D.C.)
9. Mortgage Bankers Association (Washington, D.C.)
10, 11. U.S. Department of Housing and Urban Development (Washington, D.C.)
12. Aspen/Pitkin County Housing Office (Aspen, Colo.)
13, 14. U.S. Department of Housing and Urban Development (Washington, D.C.)
15. Housing Assistance Council (Washington, D.C.)
16, 17. The Brookings Institution (Washington, D.C.)
18. U.S. Department of Agriculture (Washington, D.C.)

VACATION

HOLIDAYS

1. *The World Almanac and Book of Facts 1996*, World Almanac Books (Mahwah, N.J.)
2. The First Lady's Press Office/Federation of American Scientists (Washington, D.C.)
3. The Tabernacle Church (Laurel, Md.)
4. The Church of Scientology (N.Y.C.)

5. Ronald Hutton,*The Rise and Fall of Merry England*, Oxford University Press (London, England)
6. U.S. Consumer Product Safety Commission (Bethesda, Md.)

7, 8. Joel Best, University of Delaware (Newark)

9. Center for Science in the Public Interest (Washington, D.C.)
10. Centers for Disease Control and Prevention (Atlanta)
11. Butterball Turkey Talkline (Downers Grove, Ill.)
12. Cyber Dialogue (N.Y.C.)

13, 14. American Dairy Association (Rosemont, Ill.)

15. Franklin Mills Mall (Philadelphia)

16–19. Macy's (N.Y.C.)

20, 21. Marriott Marquis (N.Y.C.)

TRAVEL AND TOURISM

1. Cunard Lines (N.Y.C.)
2. The National Trust for Places of Historic or Natural Beauty (London, England)
3. The Business Card Museum (Erdenheim, Pa.)
4. Amusement Business (Nashville)

5, 6. Transylvanian Society of Dracula (St. John's, Newfoundland)

7. Fox News/Opinion Dynamics poll (N.Y.C.)
8. Intuitive Vision Network (Long Island, N.Y.)
9. The Cruise Authority (Marietta, Ga.)
10. International Transport Workers' Federation (London, England)
11. Club Med, Inc. (N.Y.C.)
12. Government of India Tourist Office (N.Y.C.)
13. Sporting Goods Manufacturers Association (North Palm Beach, Fla.)
14. http://www.nbc.com
15. The Washington Hilton Hotel (Washington, D.C.)
16. National Park Service (Washington, D.C.)
17. Madame Tussaud's Wax Museum (Sydney, Australia)
18. Tochigi Prefectural Government (Utsunomiya City, Japan)
19. George Washington's Mount Vernon (Va.)
20. Conner Prairie Museum (Indianapolis)
21. Lower East Side Tenement Museum (N.Y.C.)
22. Obertraun Tourism (Obertraun, Austria)
23. The Venetian (Las Vegas, Nev.)/Associazione Veneziana Albergatori (Venice, Italy)
24. Inston Design International (London, England)

THE SPORTING LIFE

1. *Harper's* research
2. American Bowling Congress/Women's International Bowling Congress/Young American Bowling Alliance (Greendale, Wis.)
3. Sporting Goods Manufacturers Association (North Palm Beach, Fla.)
4. *Sportsman's Guide* (St. Paul, Minn.)
5. NBA Store (N.Y.C)
6, 7. *Sports Illustrated* (N.Y.C.)
8. ABC Sports/NBC Sports (N.Y.C.)
9, 10. Paul Bernhardt, Georgia State University (Atlanta)
11. Texas University Interscholastic League (Austin)
12, 13. National Spit Tobacco Education Program (Chicago)
14. Novartis Pharmaceuticals Corporation (East Hanover, N.J.)
15. National Basketball Association (N.Y.C.)
16. Research Institute on Addictions (Buffalo, N.Y.)
17. James "Bubba" Ball (Columbus, Ga.)
18. United States Golf Association (Far Hills, N.J.)
19. National Sporting Goods Association (Mount Prospect, Ill.)
20. Grants Management Office (Atlanta)
21–23. Atlanta Committee for the Olympic Games
24. *Fortune* (N.Y.C.)
25. Spike Lee/Madison Square Garden (N.Y.C.)
26. Denver Buffalo Company
27–30. Sporting Goods Manufacturers Association (North Palm Beach, Fla.)
31. Indianapolis Motor Speedway/Goodyear (Akron)
32. New Jersey Pest Control Association (Cherry Hill, N.J.)
33. Great American Duck Race of Deming, Inc. (Deming, N.Mex.)
34. *St. Petersburg Times* (Moscow, Russia)
35. Yukigassen International Snow Battle Contest (Kemijarvi, Finland)
36. The Danish Institute for Clinical Epidemiology (Copenhagen, Denmark)
37. Mike Easterbrook, University of Toronto (Ontario)
38. United Media (N.Y.C.)

THE GREAT OUTDOORS

1. Green Graphics (Russellville, Ky.)
2. U.S. Geological Survey (Reston, Va.)
3, 4. W. T. Frankenberger Jr., University of California at Riverside
5. Ford Motor Company (Dearborn, Mich.)
6. Yosemite National Park (Yosemite, Calif.)
7. National Parks and Conservation Association (Washington, D.C.)
8. National Forest Service (Denver)

9. Minnesota Department of Natural Resources/Minnesota Department of Transportation (St. Paul)
10. Center for Marine Conservation (Washington, D.C.)
11. Skelly Engineering (Encinitas, Calif.)
12. Du Pont (Wilmington, Del.)
13. Manatee County Attorney's Office (Bradenton, Fla.)

14, 15. Dole for President (Washington, D.C.)

16. *Consumer Reports* (Yonkers, N.Y.)
17. United Nations Environment Program (Nairobi, Kenya)
18. International Trade Information Service (Southwest Harbor, Maine)
19. World Conservation Union (Washington, D.C.)
20. Lincoln Correctional Center (Lincoln, Ill.)
21. Agricultural Research Service (Beltsville, Md.)
22. George Craig, University of Notre Dame (South Bend, Ind.)
23. DEJAY Corporation (Greeneville, Tenn.)

LEISURE TIME

1. Daniel A. Potter, University of Kentucky (Lexington)
2. BIC Corporation (Milford, Conn.)

3, 4. The Exploratorium (San Francisco)

5. MCI (Washington, D.C.)
6. Levi Strauss & Co. (San Francisco)
7. Bill Zehme, *The Way You Wear Your Hat: Frank Sinatra and the Lost Art of Livin'*, HarperCollins (N.Y.C.)
8. *Who's Who in Central Banking*, Central Banking Publications (London, England)
9. Sporting Goods Manufacturers Association (North Palm Beach, Fla.)
10. U.S. Lawn Mower Racing Association (Glenview, Ill.)
11. Bubbles Capitol Hill (Washington, D.C.)
12. *Harper's* research
13. Fox News/Opinion Dynamics poll (N.Y.C)
14. Office of the Vice President/The *Washington Post* (Washington, D.C.)
15. Triarch Beverage Group (White Plains, N.Y.)
16. Orlando Magic (Orlando, Fla.)

JUNK FOOD

1. Kellogg Co. (Battle Creek, Mich.)
2. U.S. District Court for the Northern District of Texas (Dallas)
3. Rocky's Mountain Oysters (Denver)
4. Navy Office of Information, East (N.Y.C.)

5. House of Assembly (Hamilton, Bermuda)
6. Golin/Harris International (Washington, D.C.)
7, 8. McDonald's Corporation (Oak Brook, Ill.)
9, 10. Kraft Foods Inc. (White Plains, N.Y.)
11. Patrice Tanaka & Company (N.Y.C.)/Chocolate Manufacturers Association (McLean, Va.)
12. San Diego County Office of the Public Administrator/Guardian
13. Vidalia (Washington, D.C.)
14, 15. Donuts (Randolph, Mass.)
16. Pegi Waffle (Santa Ana, Calif.)
17, 18. Toledo Police Department (Ohio)

SEX

1. The Andrology Institute (Lexington, Ky.)
2. Harlequin Enterprises, Ltd. (Don Mills, Ontario)
3, 4. Beverly Hills Center for Sexual Medicine (Calif.)
5. Cowen & Co. (N.Y.C.)
6. *Penthouse* (N.Y.C.)
7. Bear, Stearns & Co. Inc. (N.Y.C.)
8. U.S. Department of Defense (Arlington, Va.)
9, 10. Alan Hirsch, Smell & Taste Research and Treatment Foundation (Chicago)
11. Craig Freeman (Ventura, Calif.)
12, 13. American Civil Liberties Union (N.Y.C.)
14. *Harper's* research
15, 16. Office of Representative Tom Coburn (Washington, D.C.)
17. Park E. Dietz (Newport Beach, Calif.)
18. *Marietta Daily Journal* (Marietta, Ga.)
19. *Journal of the American Medical Association* (Chicago)
20. *Feminism and Psychology* (London, England)
21. Meadows, Ichter & Trigg (Atlanta)
22. Myriad Public Relations (Cambridge, England)
23. Kevis of Beverly Hills (Calif.)
24. Kinky Joe's Erotic Furniture, Inc. (N.Y.C.)
25–27. James R. Petersen, *The Century of Sex*, Grove Press (N.Y.C.)
28. Athan G. Theoharis, *J. Edgar Hoover, Sex, and Crime: An Historical Antidote*, Ivan R. Dee, Inc. (Chicago)
29. Fox Family Channel (Los Angeles)/Michael McLean & Associates (Studio City, Calif.)
30. NBC Sports (N.Y.C.)
31. University of Nebraska State Museum (Lincoln)

Index

Index